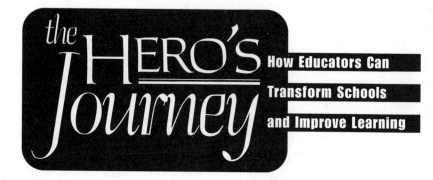

the HERO'S Journey

How Educators Can
Transform Schools
and Improve Learning

John L. Brown and Cerylle A. Moffett

ASCD

Association for Supervision
and Curriculum Development

Alexandria, Virginia USA

Association for Supervision and Curriculum Development
1703 N. Beauregard St. • Alexandria, VA 22311-1714 USA
Telephone: 1-800-933-2723 or 703-578-9600 • Fax: 703-575-5400
Web site: http://www.ascd.org • E-mail: member@ascd.org

Gene R. Carter, *Executive Director*

Michelle Terry, *Associate Executive Director, Program Development*

Nancy Modrak, *Director, Publishing*

John O'Neil, *Director of Acquisitions*

Julie Houtz, *Managing Editor of Books*

Carolyn R. Pool, *Associate Editor*

Charles D. Halverson, *Project Assistant*

Gary Bloom, *Director, Design and Production Services*

Karen Monaco, *Senior Designer*

Tracey A. Smith, *Production Manager*

Dina Murray, *Production Coordinator*

John Franklin, *Production Coordinator*

Cynthia Stock, *Desktop Publisher*

Robert Land, *Indexer*

Printed in the United States of America.

July 1999 member book (pc). ASCD Premium, Comprehensive, and Regular members periodically receive ASCD books as part of their membership benefits. No. FY99-8.

ASCD Stock No. 199002   ASCD member price: $16.95; nonmember price: $20.95

Library of Congress Cataloging-in-Publication Data
Brown, John L., 1947–
    The hero's journey : how educators can transform schools and
Improve learning / John L. Brown and Cerylle A. Moffett.
        p.   cm.
    Includes bibliographical references (p.) and index.
    ISBN 0-87120-344-8 (pbk.)
    1. School improvement programs—United States.   2. Educational
change—United States.   3. Educators—United States Interviews.   I.
Moffett, Cerylle A., 1942–   II. Title.
    LB2822.82 .B76   1999
    371.2'00973—dc21   99-6342
                                                                           CIP

04 03 02 01 00 99   10 9 8 7 6 5 4 3 2 1

THE HERO'S JOURNEY: HOW EDUCATORS CAN TRANSFORM SCHOOLS AND IMPROVE LEARNING

ACKNOWLEDGMENTS

We would first like to acknowledge the generosity of the colleagues who agreed to be interviewed for this book. They were willing to take time from demanding professional and personal responsibilities to sit with us and share their thoughts on the phases of the hero's journey. They communicated with us in person, by phone, by fax, by e-mail, and by notes of encouragement as they shared their own experience of the hero's journey at the school, district, and national levels.

Thus, we gratefully acknowledge the friends and colleagues (teachers, principals, district-level administrators, and national education consultants) who allowed us to interview them for this book: Linda Adamson, Barrie Bennett, Russ Claus, Marcie Emberger, Barbara Graves, Tony Gregorc, Sheila Jackson, Kathy Kurtz, Tom Lafovore, Constance Manter, Mary McDonnough, Lorraine Monroe, Diana Pearson, Jan Stocklinski, Mikki Terry, Ann Walker, and Tom Whitaker.

Other colleagues were also there to lend support and encouragement. In particular, we would like to acknowledge Antoinette Kellaher, Kathleen Fitzpatrick, Gayle Gregory, Carol Rolheiser, and Joanne Quinn. Our shared conversations sustained us, helped us stay on course, reaffirmed our belief in the power of collaborative inquiry, and allowed us to check and recheck our vision against the reality of life in schools, districts, and the national education arena.

We would especially like to thank our ASCD editors and other staff members for their professionalism and dedication to this book. We are also indebted to Allene Chriest and Susan McConville for their outstanding administrative support. Finally, we are grateful to our extended families—for their encouragement, their faith in us, and their prayers: We give thanks and love to Laird Moffett, Mary and John Cervase, Janet Brown, Antoinette and Don Kellaher, Jonathan and Matthew Fritts, and Ken and Lisa Reinshuttle.

PREFACE

WHY THE HERO'S JOURNEY?

> The heroic educator is not an isolated, charismatic, or superhuman individual who hands down miraculous answers from on high. Instead, this is a person like us, who might say: "Come with me. We can do this together." She could be a colleague who, by virtue of being a little farther down the road, can look back and say: "I've been there, and it's not so bad around the bend. Don't worry. I know it feels pretty dark right here. But it gets light up ahead."
>
> —INTERVIEW WITH A TEACHER OF THE YEAR

Why This Book?

Individual and shared acts of heroism have inspired courage and hope throughout the ages in every corner of our globe. Heroes have changed the course of history. Some have become the subjects of myth, art, film, and legend. Others have acted quietly—known only to those whose lives they have touched. In the United States today, we are at a crossroads in education that calls for nothing less than heroism. Our current structures for schooling are exhausted. They make it "agonizingly difficult" (Hargreaves & Fullan, 1998) for educators at all levels to respond to the needs of children in a global society. Regardless of efforts to develop state and local standards, new forms of assessment, innovations in technology, or applications of new approaches to teaching and learning, these attempts at educational reform will not succeed without fundamental and heroic changes in the culture, structures, policies, and perceptions of the place we call school.

According to cultural anthropologist Joseph Campbell (1949), in times of darkness and confusion that test our minds, hearts, and spirit, we have often looked to heroes of other times and places to give us courage and hope. This is such a time in the history of public education. The complexity of the current educational reform agenda demands courageous, responsible, determined action on the part of all who believe that preparing our children for life in the 21st century is both a national priority and a moral responsibility. For schools to become responsive communities of caring and of academic rigor for all students, business as usual is no longer an option. To enact change where it matters most—in the culture and instructional practices of schools—we need bold action. We must build a new coalition that includes teachers, students, administrators, support staff, parents, caregivers, businesses, service organizations, and members of local and regional communities. The times demand that we act in greater numbers with extraordinary vision, integrity, and caring for children we serve. We believe we are up to the task.

The universal myth of the heroic journey has direct relevance to educators in quest of the courage to take unprecedented action on behalf of children—to initiate fundamental change in the structure and culture of our schools. In *The Hero with a Thousand Faces,* Joseph Campbell reinforces the inspirational power of mythology: "Throughout the inhabited world, in all times and under every circumstance, the myths of man have flourished; they have been the living inspiration of whatever else may have appeared out of the activities of the human body and mind" (1949, p. 3). A prime function of mythology has always been to touch the mind and heart in powerful ways that propel the human spirit forward despite the obstacles that pull it back.

We believe that applying the conceptual lens of the archetypal heroic journey to the challenges we face in contemporary education can stimulate the personal and professional commitment needed for courageous action on the part of individuals, teams, and school communities. Metaphor has the power to kindle the imagination and touch the heart. When educators and school communities examine their beliefs and actions against the powerful metaphor of the hero's journey, the result can be increased awareness, the identification of shared purpose, and a commitment to the urgency of action. The call is to create schools capable of nurturing the intellectual potential, igniting the imagination, and developing the character of each and every student.

We also believe that the potential for heroism lives within each of us, waiting to be realized. To rise to the call for heroic action means that, regardless of external obstacles and internal tests of fortitude, we each accept the responsibility and sustain the commitment for confronting and resolving the complex problems that face administrators, teachers, and students in schools today. Heroic members of educational communities are like the heroes of Campbell's universal myth.

They are the men and the women who are able to battle past their personal, cultural, and limitations to a higher form of humanity. They give themselves to a cause greater than themselves. Campbell (1949) defines the hero as

> the champion not of things become but of things becoming.
> . . . The dragon to be slain by him is precisely the monster of
> the status quo. The hero's task always has been and always
> will be to bring new life to a dying culture. (p. 20)

Who Is This Book For?

This book is for any member of an educational community—teacher, principal, staff developer, district office administrator, superintendent, professor of teacher education, parent, caregiver, or community member—who wishes to gain insight, understanding, and a clear sense of purpose regarding the most appropriate direction for educational reform. Much of the substance of the book came from interviews with just such people. We believe this book can also be used by groups (e.g., school teams; coalitions of educators, parents, and community members) as a research-based tool to facilitate meaningful dialogue and thoughtful consensus about ways to fundamentally transform our schools.

How Can People Use This Book?

Issues surrounding the complexity of the current educational reform agenda often touch individuals at the core of their being—that is, their belief systems. When belief systems differ, conversation becomes more difficult, and constructive dialogue often becomes impossible. We believe that the questions raised by the stages of the hero's journey can serve as a catalyst for substantive discussions in highly polarized groups. The journey metaphor can serve as a facilitation tool to help groups

- create a shared vision and the action plan needed to achieve it;
- build commitment to implement a vision that already exists; and
- initiate a rapid response to complex problems where no coordinating group, common language, or shared vision now exists.

The result of using the metaphor of the hero's journey, as it is outlined in this book, can be respectful and productive communication among diverse constituencies about the purpose and direction of schools. To stimulate this kind of dialogue, we have embedded "Reflection Checkpoints" in each chapter. We suggest that the Reflection Checkpoint questions be used in

- school-based staff development sessions,
- study groups,
- school district planning initiatives,
- community forums, and
- professional development workshops.

Educators and members of the school community can also use the checkpoints in a variety of other settings to develop informed consensus, based on research and practice, about a bold new vision for schools and the steps needed to achieve it. The metaphors embedded in the stages of the heroic journey are especially useful as catalysts for substantive dialogue among individuals with widely diverging viewpoints.

❖ ❖ ❖

Transcending time and space, and spanning the cultural diversity of civilizations around the globe, the metaphor of the hero's journey touches individuals and groups at their emotional, moral, and spiritual core. As a result, groups of educators and community members can become more aware of the forces that unite, not divide, them. Thus, we can significantly reduce the polarization that now exists in a highly politicized, emotionally charged, educational reform arena.

JOHN L. BROWN
Alexandria, Virginia

CERYLLE A. MOFFETT
Alexandria, Virginia
June 1999

INTRODUCTION

THE JOURNEY BEGINS

━━━━━━━

> We have not to risk the adventure alone, for the heroes of all
> time have gone before us. The labyrinth is thoroughly known.
> We have only to follow the thread of the heroic path, and
> where we had thought to find an abomination, we shall find a
> god. And where we had thought to slay another, we shall slay
> ourselves. Where we had thought to travel outward, we will
> come to the center of our own existence. And where we had
> thought to be alone, we will be with all the world.
>
> — JOSEPH CAMPBELL, *THE HERO WITH A THOUSAND FACES*
> (1949, p. 25)

This is a book about hope. It travels through the labyrinth of modern
education, curling and rippling out toward the promise of light. It is an
affirmation of the power and courage of shared vision, purpose, and
inquiry. Through a shared mission, we can work together to find viable
answers to the riddles of chaos and complexity troubling educators, students, parents, and community members everywhere. Above
all, it is a reminder that in the collective wisdom of myth and legend
we can find the inspiration for a heroic journey that is the destiny of all
individuals and groups working today to transform schools into
authentic learning organizations.

Each of us in a position to influence the experience of children in schools soon comes to realize that—knowingly or unknowingly—we have embarked on a spiritual, intellectual, and social journey, a quest for personal and organizational transformation in the face of mounting problems and contradictions. This book is dedicated to an understanding of this journey. We have chosen to use the archetypal story of the hero's journey, as it appears in world literature, as a controlling metaphor and symbolic framework for exploring the change process that is an inevitable part of both personal renewal and educational reform. As a state teacher of the year suggested in one of our interviews:

> We never really arrive at the point of being a hero, but we are constantly becoming heroic. We don't ever "get there." We are always "getting there." The horizons keep moving, and the needs keep evolving. What we do know is that our capacity for learning is unlimited.

Ancient and Modern Heroes

It is possible for all educators today—living in an age of unprecedented upheaval in the education reform arena—to view themselves as mythic heroes. Even if we are unaware that we are on this path, each of us is engaged in a type of mythic struggle to bring order, meaning, and purpose to times of chaos and complexity.

- Like Odysseus in *The Odyssey,* we are fighting to overcome seemingly insurmountable obstacles to reinstate stability, order, and purpose in a homeland to which forces seem determined to prevent our return.
- Like Dorothy in *The Wizard of Oz,* we are all struggling to return to a part of ourselves we appear to have lost in the face of unprecedented and unpredictable change.
- Like Luke Skywalker in *Star Wars,* we are all testing our resolve to stay the course and fight "the dark side" as we usher education into the next millennium.
- Like Dante in *The Divine Comedy,* we are searching for renewal through a pathway leading from chaos and perplexity into unity and cohesion.

- Like Arjuna in the Indian epic *The Mahabharata,* we are all struggling to find our capacity for purposeful action in the face of what appears to be overwhelming anxiety, hesitation, and confusion.
- Finally, like the Arthurian knight *Parzival,* we are all endeavoring to transcend our individual limitations, questing, instead, for the realization of a transcendental vision to guide our actions and those of our students toward deeper understanding and wisdom.

In effect, we are all heroes immersed in a quest to help our schools and school systems respond to the increasingly complex demands of the world of the Information Age. Old answers are no longer viable for the new questions we are confronting, just as old paradigms and old solutions are insufficient to respond to the new and unanticipated problems in contemporary education. We are all both individual and collaborative *questors,* searching for viable ways to transform our schools into communities of academic integrity, lifelong learning, and extraordinary caring for the children we serve. The object of our quest is the capacity to initiate, support, and sustain meaningful educational change.

Interviews with Educators: Testing the Power of Metaphor

Important "reality checks" in developing this book were the dialogue interviews we conducted with selected educators. We interviewed a representative group of educators at all levels—teachers, principals, district-level administrators, staff developers, and nationally recognized education consultants—and used the questions stimulated by each stage of the hero's journey to guide our dialogue (see Appendix A for Interview Guides and Appendix B for Extended Interviews). We were excited with the results.

From interviews with a variety of heroic educators—from a teacher of the year to a nationally recognized principal of a successful urban high school—the following themes emerged as we used the metaphor of the journey to facilitate thought and dialogue:

1. Each of our journeys in education began in a condition of untested innocence and naive unconsciousness.

2. Our naivete is shattered when we become aware of the complexity of classroom teaching and school administration. It also continues to be challenged when we are confronted by the myriad problems that must be solved if our students are to be fully prepared for life in a changing world.

3. We all have challenges and even threats on our journeys, and it is possible to be brave and imaginative enough to overcome them.

4. Our professional lives are inextricably linked with those of our students and colleagues.

5. There is enormous power and efficacy in collaborative inquiry, reflection on action, and shared decision making.

6. We all need wisdom figures, allies, and kindred spirits to help us stay the course.

7. The trials and tests we face and overcome on the journey make us stronger, more resilient, and more whole. The toughest tests are the internal ones that challenge our determination and sense of purpose.

8. Educational transformation is as much a moral and spiritual calling as it is a professional obligation.

9. Through personal responsibility, shared purpose, and collaborative and courageous action, it is possible to make a genuine difference in the lives of all our students.

As a result of the conversations that took place in the interviews, we became even more convinced that metaphor as a dialogue tool has the power to promote critical analysis, the shared construction of knowledge, and renewed commitment to action. Most important, we reaffirmed that the deep learning that comes from exploring new landscapes with trusted colleagues is indeed a social, intellectual, emotional, and spiritual act.

The metaphor of the heroic journey is so universal that it enables even highly polarized groups to find common ground, identify shared purpose, and reach consensus on informed action. Metaphor has the power to kindle the imagination and touch the heart. In so doing, it can help members of a diverse school community become more aware of the things that unite them, rather than what divides them. The result is often a higher level of creative thinking on the part of teams and a commitment to translating plans into action.

Elements of the Hero's Journey

The book is structured around three interlinking elements. First, it profiles six phases of the mythic hero's journey from unconscious innocence to ultimate self-awareness, insight, and transformation. Second, it parallels each phase with a delineation of the critical issues confronting educators today. Finally, the book investigates each phase through the voices of practicing educators, all heroic in their own ways. As we mentioned previously, the interview process offered a unique set of perspectives united by the common elements of the hero's journey.

In this introduction, we have already taken the first step, beginning our journey. Each of the following chapters profiles the stages we have identified as being part of the archetypal hero's journey, including the quest through chaos, the gurus and companions who help, the trials and initiations, and the insights gained along the way. Each chapter shows how educators can understand and navigate the hero's journey in contemporary education reform and discusses the current research and literature that relate to this journey.

Chapter 1, "Educational Transformation and the Hero's Journey," summarizes the most important themes that inform this book. It outlines the concept of the heroic journey as a symbolic framework for exploring the change process that is an inevitable part of both personal transformation and educational reform. In this chapter, we assert that each of us is engaged, even if we are unaware of it, in an archetypal struggle to bring order, meaning, and purpose to the field of modern education and school reform during times of unprecedented complexity, confusion, and change.

We define heroism in modern education as an act and process involving collective will and vision. The notion of the "Lone Ranger" working alone to restore order in a chaotic world is no longer a viable or desirable icon. Instead, we are all in this together. Supported by the literature on collaborative work cultures in schools, the heroism we speak of here involves neither miracles nor martyrdom. Educators working in isolation can, at times, perform miracles. But what is the toll, and how long can isolated heroism be sustained? When do isolated heroic educators become what Fullan (1993a) called "moral martyrs"?

We need to rethink the distinction between heroism and martyrdom, guided by the notion that informed group inquiry, dialogue, decision making, and action may have far more energy and potential for sustaining educational transformation than the isolated educator working alone.

Chapter 2, "The Philosopher's Stone: What Do We Know About Organizational Renewal and Educational Transformation?" presents an overview of the educational and organizational literature that guided and challenged our thinking as we wrote this book. In this chapter, we look at four educational implications of the current thinking in the sciences, change theory, cognitive science, and the power of myth and metaphor, as follows:

• Implications for educators and educational systems of the literature on systems thinking, chaos theory, and the "New Science"—in particular, breakthroughs in quantum physics and related disciplines that have reshaped the ways scientists are viewing the predictability and stability of our physical universe.

• Implications for educators of findings from research and practice in the most current literature on educational change, together with concepts from the organizational-renewal literature.

• Implications of new cognitive learning theory and brain research on our views of how individuals and organizations, as living systems, learn.

• The implications of using the universal themes in world mythology as conceptual filters for viewing the process of educational reform.

Chapter 3, "Innocence Lost: Breakdown Requires Breakthrough," begins the exploration of the hero's journey toward educational transformation with an investigation of the outworn models and mindsets that are still influencing our views of education. This chapter asserts that a principal outcome of our "lost innocence," which is an inevitable part of the heroic quest, is an individual and collective acknowledgment that we frequently see things through the rearview mirrors of the past rather than experiencing realistic perceptions and judgments about the present and future. This tendency to cling to outworn mental models of how education should work compounds the chaos, complexity, and discord that characterize the modern educational arena. It weaves into the narrative of the hero's journey suggestions for dealing purposefully with resistance to change and the temptation to "tinker around the edges"—to limit reform efforts to cosmetic or small-scale changes simply because these are within the range of our comfort zone.

Chapter 4, "Chaos and Complexity This Way Come: Confronting the Dragon at the Door and the Serpent in the Garden," extends the exploration of rearview mirror thinking into other arenas involving problems, barriers, issues, and undeclared realities that make it essential for us to embark on the heroic journey in education today. Specifically, what is forcing us collectively to take our heads out of the metaphorical sand? What is the nature of the dragon at the door and the serpent in the garden that necessitates immediate and dramatic educational change? Paralleling the threat of such mythic adversaries are modern hazards:

- Currently held, albeit outdated, models of teaching and learning.
- Industrial models of administration and supervision.
- Simplistic and counterproductive approaches to professional development.
- Failure to understand the phenomenon of organizational culture in relation to change.
- Inadequate concepts of technology and its uses.
- Incomplete approaches to school-to-career transitioning in a world of unprecedented economic and social change.

This chapter also explores Ralph Stacey's (1996) notion of the "shadow organization," that is, social, political, and interpersonal actions that go on under the table—outside the rules of the "legitimate" system—and that can wreak havoc in school systems if they are not brought to the surface and acknowledged as real.

Chapter 5, "The Heroic Quest: The Search for the Grail, the Jewel in the Lotus, and Avalon," explores the following essential questions:

- What exactly are we searching for in modern education?
- What is the vision that is driving our quest?
- What is making it impossible for us to remain in the comfort of the known and familiar?

- What are we individually and collectively committed to discovering about ourselves and about how to make schools work as heroic learning organizations?

This chapter addresses these questions within the metaphor of the hero's journey, asking readers to consider what they themselves are searching for as educators and what they are willing to help their schools and school systems become and achieve. The heroic quest in education includes a search for common standards and controlling values, including ways to ensure that curriculum, instruction, and assessment are vital, aligned, and mutually supportive processes. It also entails a search for ways to integrate the best of what we now know about the learning process so as to guarantee that our children have an educational experience based on the principles of excellence and equity for all students.

Chapter 6, "Gurus and Alliances: Companions Along the Way," explores an inevitable part of the hero's journey—the need to reach out to companions of like heart and mind. This outreach involves the hero's search for connections with like-minded colleagues, as well as with wisdom figures—individuals and groups who embody insight and expert knowledge. This chapter focuses on how the ideas of educational reform leaders and theorists on excellent teaching (and the need for collaborative work cultures to support it) can bring light to the dark periods of the hero's quest. It points out the need for external knowledge to eventually become internalized as personal wisdom and insight. In effect, the *novice* must become the *initiate;* what was once embodied in the physical form of gurus or mentors and their teachings becomes a part of the collective wisdom of heroes and their shires, kingdoms, or communities.

This chapter acknowledges that a vast and untapped source of professional knowledge lies within each school in the form of the collective craft knowledge of its teachers. As confirmed by our interviews, many educators—when asked about their gurus and mentors—do not cite nationally recognized "experts." Rather, they mention time and again that their most valued mentor was a trusted professional colleague—someone from *within* their school, organization, or professional network of colleagues.

Chapter 7, "Trials, Tests, and Initiations: Staying the Course," describes how the hero of myth, folklore, and legend inevitably undergoes a series of major tests and initiations, which, at first, appear both insurmountable and externalized. Ultimately, however, the heroes realize that these trials are a necessary and inevitable part of their personal growth and transformation. The ultimate tests are the internal ones. This chapter explores the most common problems and pressing demands facing schools as they attempt to initiate change today and suggests several solutions. It looks at the reasons why "problems can be our friends" (Fullan & Miles, 1992) when implementing change and why, counterintuitively, more is to be gained by "moving toward the danger" (Hargreaves & Fullan, 1998).

Chapter 8, "Insight and Transformation: Arriving Where We Started and Knowing the Place for the First Time," synthesizes the major insights and implications of the hero's journey from the perspective of what it means to be a heroic educator, a heroic school, and a heroic school system. It provides guidelines that others might use as they consider their own journeys. This chapter also examines ways to transform learning in the heroic school and how educators can forge a collective commitment to ensure that all learners demonstrate both independence and interdependence. In equipping the learner—whether a student, teacher, administrator, or parent/community member—with the capacity for developing and demonstrating lifelong habits of mind, the heroic school must ultimately become an inclusive community of lifelong learners—a community characterized by academic rigor, professional excellence, and extraordinary caring for the welfare of each child it serves.

Finally, the **Epilogue,** "Coming Full Circle," provides suggestions for ways educators can use the ideas and principles we present in this book. For example, educators can use the ideas presented here to self-assess and reflect on their own path from innocence to experience. School staffs, particularly school improvement teams, can use these ideas to enrich and expand dialogue and strategic planning related to improving both staff and student performance. Finally, at the system level, stakeholders can use the metaphor of the heroic journey as the theme for districtwide forums that involve administrators, teachers, students, parents, and community members in substantive, informed dialogue about a shared vision for educational reform—and the steps needed to get there.

❖ ❖ ❖

The power of metaphor as a catalyst for dialogue is that it engages not only the intellect but the heart, the values, and the deep aspirations of all participants. Above all, this is a book about a shared journey that all who care about the future of education can embark on—a journey that can transform the lives of our "fellow travelers" and the children entrusted to our care.

1

EDUCATIONAL TRANSFORMATION
AND THE HERO'S JOURNEY

Some people spend a lifetime attempting to live according to
cultural images that never quite fit them. . . . Whenever a
knight of the Grail tried to follow a path made by someone
else, he went altogether astray. Where there is a way or path, it
is someone else's footsteps. Each of us has to find our own
way. . . .

—JOSEPH CAMPBELL, *CREATIVE MYTHOLOGY* (1968, p. 4)

The road was new to me,
as roads always are,
going back. . . .

— SARAH ORNE JEWETT
(quoted in *THE QUOTABLE TRAVELER*, 1994, p. 125)

The hero's journey that is the metaphorical framework for this book
arises from a long, rich, and universal tradition involving the literature
of self-discovery, personal inquiry, and organizational renewal. Although the concept of the journey is timeless, with its roots in each of
the ancient wisdom teachings associated with various early world civilizations, its academic origins begin with the work of James George
Frazer and his classic study of the archetypal beliefs and mythic patterns of humanity, *The Golden Bough* (1994/1890). Frazer's work has

influenced subsequent discourse, both literary and psychological, on the ancient hero's journey. *The Golden Bough* has informed the psychoanalytical traditions of Freud and Jung and the literary concept of the meta-myth, that is, a single powerful archetype of the hero's path toward enlightenment, espoused by Joseph Campbell (1949).

Origins and Archetypes

Frazer began this tradition by providing a lens for examining the mythic hero as a manifestation of humanity's struggle to bring order out of chaos through the power of mythic narrative.

For Frazer, a hero is any individual (male or female) who transcends the norms of a group to embody the highest moral virtues reflected in the collective vision of the universe shared by the members of that group. The hero begins in a state of innocence and unconsciousness and ends in a state of grace and higher consciousness. The hero demonstrates, throughout the transformation process, a sustained commitment to ideals that represents the best to which anyone in the group can aspire. As part of the pathway to heroic transformation, Frazer and other writers in this tradition affirm, the hero always undergoes a series of tests and initiations that require moral courage, fortitude, assembled resources, and external support through companions along the way. The hero is ultimately an earthly manifestation of transcendental and enduring universal principles and patterns in human experience.

Sigmund Freud and Carl Jung integrated facets of the hero's journey into their groundbreaking work with modern psychoanalysis. Freud, for example, introduced the concept of the dream symbol as a projection of unconscious but felt elements of human experience. The symbols that populate our nighttime landscape can teach us, Freud asserted, about ourselves and our struggle to become conscious beings. Freud's partner, Carl Jung, extended the notion of the individual symbol into the concept of the *archetype:* universal, symbolic patterns that are found in all major world religions, mythological systems, and worldviews. According to Jung:

> The concept of the archetype . . . is derived from the repeated observation that . . . the myths and fairy tales of world

literature contain definite motifs which crop up everywhere.
. . . They have their origin in the archetype, which in itself is an
irrepresentable, unconscious, pre-existent form that seems to
be part of the inherited structure of the psyche and can therefore manifest itself spontaneously anywhere, at any time.
(Storr, 1983, p. 415)

Joseph Campbell's famous work *The Hero with a Thousand Faces*
(1949) describes the archetypal hero's journey as a series of interconnecting phases that have shaped much of contemporary thinking on
the subject. Beginning in a state of idyllic innocence and unconsciousness, the hero or heroine eventually confronts some external embodiment of discord or evil. In choosing to embark on the path of
adventure, heroes confront not only external barriers but their own
undeveloped nature. Ultimately, through a series of trials and tests, heroes overcome the forces of darkness and bring a gift to their world
that results in its transformation.

We also see the presence of the hero's journey in educational settings. In a 3rd grade classroom in San Francisco, for example, a heroic
teacher helps economically disadvantaged students engage in hands-
on science experiments, using a rich variety of manipulatives to de-
duce scientific principles about ecosystems. Similarly, heroism is present in a faculty meeting in Chicago, when a middle school action
research team reveals its recommendations for solving the problem of
student underachievement in reading and mathematics, as measured
by state-mandated tests. The rest of the staff applaud as they realize
that this seven-member team of their colleagues has broken through
seemingly insurmountable barriers to describe a workable solution to
critical site-based problems. They have found a pathway toward the
light and a passageway out of a perceived darkness. The hero's journey is present in all educational settings when the power of shared inquiry and commitment overcomes despair and leads to possibility and
hopefulness.

Connecting the Hero's Journey to the World of Education

Why should educators be concerned with this metaphor of the hero's
journey? One answer is that the wisdom embodied in this mythic tradi-

tion, personified in the wildly disparate shapes and events comprising the lives of the great heroic archetypes, can guide and inform our thinking and bring us back to a part of ourselves from which we may feel alienated, estranged, or even lost (see Figure 1.1 for a graphic depiction of this journey—and this book). As Campbell (1974) notes, "Mythological symbols touch and exhilarate centers of life beyond the reach of the vocabularies of reason and coercion" (p. 3).

Today, we all face incredibly difficult, demanding times in the field of education. The forces of change and complexity pervade virtually every part of our professional lives. Like every mythic hero, we are inextricably drawn into the labyrinth; like every archetypal voyager, we must find our way out of darkness and back to a more powerful and sustaining light. Our universe, like that of heroes and heroines of legend and myth, is riddled with irony, paradox, and either/or thinking:

Figure 1.1
The Hero's Journey: A Spiral of Growth

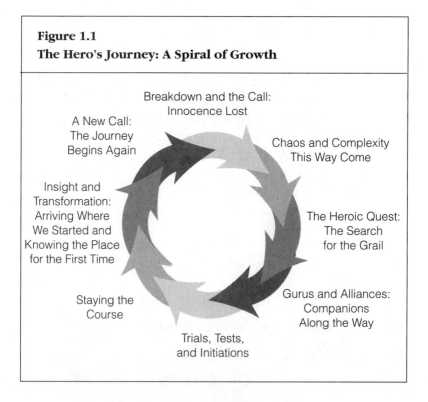

Breakdown and the Call:
Innocence Lost

A New Call:
The Journey
Begins Again

Chaos and Complexity
This Way Come

Insight and
Transformation:
Arriving Where
We Started and
Knowing the Place
for the First Time

The Heroic Quest:
The Search
for the Grail

Staying the
Course

Gurus and Alliances:
Companions
Along the Way

Trials, Tests,
and Initiations

- the contradictions of conservative and liberal viewpoints operating simultaneously while vying for supremacy in public education today;
- the controversy about pedagogical models such as whole language and phonics;
- the political demand for uniform educational standards coming at a time when pluralism, diversity, and regional autonomy have never been more powerful;
- the almost universal experience of getting a computer laboratory up and running in a school, only to find out one week later that its hardware and software are already outmoded;
- the persistent call for individualization of instruction, coupled with an equally strong demand for organizational consistency, uniformity, and control;
- the confusion and debate over the merits and limitations of ability grouping existing side by side with passionate calls for inclusive classrooms; and
- the heightened public pressure, criticism, and concern over the failures of urban schools that have resulted in a focus on stringent accountability and sanctions, rather than support for the repair of aging buildings and a provision of quality instructional materials and increased teacher and administrator professional development.

Above all, at the heart of the heroic journey in public education is the growing need to overcome the myriad student-centered challenges confronting schools and school systems today. Just listing them can reinforce the daunting nature of school transformation; at the same time, considering these problems can reaffirm both our individual and collective need to work together as allies to realize a shared vision and purpose.

How, for example, can we ensure that we successfully address the needs of an increasingly diverse, multicultural population? In the face of sharp divisions between economic haves and have-nots, how do we provide a level playing field for all our students? Of all the economic dichotomies in education, perhaps the most challenging is the use of educational technology. How can we ensure that all students master the competencies required for success in a change-dominated, technology-driven world? In our search for equity and excellence, we also face the challenge of transforming urban infrastructures to ensure that state-of-the-art educational facilities and both human and material resources are available to all students. Combine these issues with the effects of media saturation, adolescent violence, and the growing search for shared values and norms, and you find a convincing argument for reexamining educational change today in relationship to the archetypal principles of the hero's journey.

In our collective heroic journey in education, facing chaos and complexity involves supreme truth telling. It requires that we recognize, without flinching, the dragons at our gates and the serpents in our gardens. If a Minotaur exists at the center of the labyrinth, we must confront it—and acknowledge it is a part of us. The realities of education—from the information explosion to the demands of a transient, increasingly diverse society to the ultimate need to put to rest old mental models of how schools and learning should function—require that we confront head-on our own hero's journey and abandon the condition described by the Irish poet W. B. Yeats in his poem "The Second Coming": "The best lack all conviction, while the worst are full of passionate intensity."

Initiation—the experience of being tried and tested by forces seemingly more powerful than our individual ego states—is also an inevitable part of the hero's journey. Mythic heroes tend to receive transcendental or supernatural intervention from a rich variety of gods, goddesses, genies, and myriad spirit figures. Often this aid comes in the form of amulets, or magic tokens, designed to facilitate the hero's transformation. Although the modern educator's interventions take more earthbound forms, the challenges confronting us today in the educational forest require that we use all available "amulets" that have proven effective in transforming education, particularly in locales characterized by diversity and disadvantage. Though certainly not "magic bullets," these interventions include such diverse practices as constructivist teaching and learning; action research and reflective practice; study groups and job-embedded staff development; shared decision making and problem solving; top-down/bottom-up approaches to vision development, goal setting, action planning, and implementation; and technology-driven instructional and organizational enhancements.

Ultimately, the hero's destiny leads to transformation and renewal. The heroic journey in education parallels the multifaceted journey of all mythic heroes: In the face of complacency, chaos, complexity, and an unpredictable future, heroes search for equilibrium, homeostasis, order, and peace—existential conditions that we can achieve if we are willing to undertake the quest. What is our *quest* as educational heroes? Essentially, our quest is to become more self-aware and efficacious as individuals at the interpersonal, organizational, and systemic levels. And each time we hear the call and begin the journey again, we will be doing so with a higher level of self-knowledge and a deeper and more reverent understanding of the individuals, community, and world around us.

An Expanded View of Heroism

If we approach myths superficially, the heroic myths may suggest that the archetypal hero or heroine is often a solitary person—a knight in shining armor or a Joan of Arc. We need to amplify this picture to suggest that contemporary heroism resides both in individuals and in groups working together. Collaboration is essential for the kind of personal learning that the heroic journey requires. As Fullan (1993a) notes: "There is a ceiling effect on how much we can learn if we keep to ourselves" (p. 17).

We likewise assert that to transform education, it is no longer smart to work alone. In trying to go it alone, the hero can easily become a martyr—or an egomaniac. The isolated charismatic hero or heroine can bring about change that lasts only as long as he or she does. As E. C. Murphy (1994) aptly notes in *Forging the Heroic Organization:*

> The idealized definition of a hero describes a legendary or divine figure who possesses great strength, skill, and courage. This figure, like Superman, can leap tall buildings in a single bound and can outrun a speeding locomotive. In our all-too-real world, however, even Superman will stumble, fall to temptation, and find Mike Wallace knocking on his door with a *60 Minutes* video camera whirring behind his shoulder. (p. ix)

We desperately need heroes today, but not the idealized heroes of yesterday. We need the authentic heroes of tomorrow.

To take the hero's journey is to expose ourselves to risk and opportunity. It is to open ourselves to the possibilities of hope and despair. It is a vehicle for helping students discover the best in themselves, in others, and in the world they inhabit. The challenge of contemporary education is to regain a sense of shared purpose and to recognize, all over again, the power of the learning process in transforming lives.

The beauty, complexity, and occasional terror of the hero's journey in education find powerful parallels in countless prose and verse classics. Some of these are captured in a charming book, *The Quotable Traveler* (1994). For example, this book quotes American writer Diane Ackerman: "[The journey] began in mystery, and it will end in mystery, but what a savage and beautiful country lies in between!" (p. 103).*

---

*The Quotable Traveler. Copyright 1994 by the Running Press, Philadelphia, Pennsylvania.

2

THE PHILOSOPHER'S STONE

WHAT DO WE KNOW ABOUT ORGANIZATIONAL RENEWAL AND EDUCATIONAL TRANSFORMATION?

Organizational systems succeed . . . [and] are innovative or creative . . . when they are sustained far from equilibrium in states of bounded instability. The central message of the "new science" for business people is this: Organizations are feedback systems generating such complex behavior that cause-and-effect links are broken. Therefore, no individual can intend the future of that system or control its journey to that future. Instead, what happens to an organization is created by and emerges from the self-organizing interaction between its people. The key question managers face, then, is not how to maintain stable equilibrium, but how to establish sufficient constrained instability to provoke complex learning.

—RALPH STACEY, *MANAGING THE UNKNOWABLE* (1992, p. 12)

We know a lot of people who know a lot about transforming organizations. It *has* been done. I've been in schools that work. I just don't believe that it's rocket science at this point. But this is how it feels to many educators—that we are asking the impossible.

—INTERVIEW WITH A TEACHER OF THE YEAR

In the traditions of ancient alchemy, the embodiment of personal insight and wisdom is known as the "philosopher's stone." Although superficially the catalyst with which alchemists sought to turn baser metals into gold, this stone's deeper significance lies in its representation of the unity, wholeness, and integration within human experience that results from engaging in the process of self-inquiry, exploration, and individuation. According to psychoanalyst Carl Jung:

> An old Arabian alchemist, Morienus, said: "This thing [the philosopher's stone] is extracted from you; you are its mineral, and one can find it in you." The alchemical stone (the lapis) symbolizes something that can never be lost or dissolved, something eternal. (Jung, *Man and His Symbols*, 1964, p. 226)

What is the philosopher's stone that underlies the ideas in this book? How is it possible that the great archetypes of world mythology can help to guide and inform our personal and collective journeys toward educational transformation? What have we learned from the new research on change? What can the business literature tell us about systems thinking and organizational renewal? How do the most recent findings from cognitive science and brain research relate to organizational learning?

This chapter provides a starting point for the journey and a foundation for understanding the major sources that shaped our thinking as we conceptualized this book. It outlines the ideas of theorists and practitioners that we believe can inform the individual, school, and systemic hero's journey. In particular, we looked at the work of educational researchers and practitioners, together with the work of organizational leadership specialists, with the goal of creating a new synthesis.

The New Science, Chaos Theory, and Systems Thinking

An essential part of the philosopher's stone that undergirds this book is the emerging scientific view that the universe is essentially holographic. Every part, in effect, reflects some greater and ultimately unified whole. To explore the world of the New Science is to discover striking parallels to the world of the hero's journey:

- a confirmation of an essential unity underlying the complexity of physical experience;
- an affirmation that in the face of chaos and complexity, we can discover a tapestry of interconnections and order transcending the world of paradox and opposites;
- a reminder that in the face of the limitations of space and time there are transcendent and enduring truths superseding that continuum of matter; and
- an assurance that within the dynamic, relentlessly changing, tangible universe, there are patterns, points of interpenetration, and unifying principles that can sustain the journey through turbulence.

Most intriguing is the notion that breakthroughs in learning frequently occur when we are at the edge of chaos. As Margaret Wheatley (1992) states in *Leadership and the New Science:*

> Disorder can be a source of order . . . and growth is found in disequilibrium, not in balance. The things we fear most in organizations—fluctuations, disturbances, imbalances—need not be signs of an impending disorder that will destroy us. Instead, fluctuations are the primary source of creativity. . . . The most chaotic of systems never goes beyond certain boundaries; it stays contained within a shape that we can recognize as the system's strange attractor. . . . Throughout the universe, then, order exists within disorder, and disorder within order. (pp. 20–21)

When we enter this new scientific paradigm, we are struck by an *Alice in Wonderland* feeling of down being up, of the familiar becoming strange and oddly compelling. Basic matter, for example, assumes a dual nature, appearing as either a particle or wave: This phenomenon effectively eliminates the capacity of scientists to arrive at single or absolute interpretations of manifesting phenomena. As Wheatley notes, this shift moves us, therefore, from a conceptual world of "thingness" to a world composed of energy that comes from relationships. Like the shifting landscapes of a great mythic hero's journey—enchanted castles and underworld labyrinths that emerge and then disappear—matter becomes a momentary manifestation of interacting fields that are intangible, insubstantial, and always in transition.

Yet these mutable phenomena lead, inexorably, to field boundaries, stability, and ultimate order, a condition physicists call "strange attractors" (Gleick, 1987).

A World of Paradox

At the heart of the hero's journey in education is another essential part of the philosopher's stone for this book—the storyteller's paradox that though the hero's quest must be told in linear and chronological terms, it represents multiple dimensions and has complex meanings. Like the paradoxes cited by quantum physics, the hero's journey is, in reality, a spiraling, recursive, and elliptical process. Like a three-dimensional Chinese checkers or tic-tac-toe game, multiple dimensions operate simultaneously. This phenomenon occurs both within mythic heroes' journeys and their parallels in the world of education, as embodied by the heroic individual, the heroic school, and the heroic school system.

The paradigm we are presenting is a holographic one: All of its parts reflect the whole, and vice versa—or as ancient philosophers consistently affirmed: As above, so below. The hero's journey confirms that what appear to be outliers, disconnects, or elements of separation within education are part of some greater—and perhaps unperceived—whole that is manifesting itself in the guise of chaos and complexity.

Other paradoxes embedded in the hero's journey for educators include the following: the movement of educators between the polarities of hope and despair; the recurrent phenomenon of students, parents, administrators, and teachers' demonstrating surprising resilience in the face of unprecedented change and rising demands while periodically giving in to fatigue and burnout; and the inevitable tension that comes with change as learning organizations grow.

Dealing with paradox and being able to view apparent contradictions as opposite sides of the same coin are just a few of the skills required on the heroic journey. As Fullan (1993a) notes, being involved in educational change challenges one's ability to work with polar opposites. Thus, our philosopher's stone also involves the following paradoxes:

- simultaneously pushing for change while allowing self-learning to unfold;

- making detailed plans while preparing for a journey of uncertainty;
- seeing problems as threats and also as sources of creative resolution;
  - having a vision, but not being blinded by it;
  - valuing the individual and the group simultaneously;
  - being internally cohesive, but externally oriented; and
  - valuing personal change as the route to system change.

Fractals, the Butterfly Effect, and the Journey Toward Educational Change

At the heart of the philosopher's stone that shapes the hero's journey is the awareness of the implicit beauty and order to be found within the seeming chaos of the universe we inhabit. A powerful visual image cited consistently in New Science literature reinforces this element of our philosopher's stone: the phenomenon of fractals. Fractals are beautiful geometric shapes that emerge when nonlinear equations are looped back on themselves using computer enhancement. When we understand fractals, we understand how they can become a metaphor for the heroic journey.

Like the mythic hero's experience, fractals remind us that from small changes and leverage points, large, sweeping, and beautifully holistic results occur. The fractal also underscores the potential and need for hope as we embark on the heroic journey in education. As these beautiful shapes remind us, despite the apparent chaos and complexity that pervade modern education today, we can find an ultimate beauty, order, and pattern if we continue the journey with tenacity, an open mind, discrimination, and integrity.

Another significant parallel between the hero's journey and the New Science can be found in the work of research meteorologist Edward Lorenz (1993). His famous construct of "The Butterfly Effect" suggests that we are not islands unto ourselves. As Lorenz describes this phenomenon, when a butterfly flaps its wings in Hawaii, its impact can ultimately set off a typhoon in Japan. Lorenz's acknowledgment of the interconnectedness of seemingly random physical manifestations reminds us that within the heroic journey in education, everything we do has immediate as well as long-range and often imperceptible effects on the entire system within which we operate.

Lorenz's model implies that, contrary to our inclination to decry our powerlessness, everything we do is affecting everything and everyone else within our system, regardless of how difficult it may be for us to see at the time. We can never be entirely certain of where our reach extends. We influence students in myriad, unperceived ways that affect them and the lives of people with whom they interact like the widening circles extending from a stone tossed into a tranquil pond.

Strange Attractors: Signs of Hope on the Hero's Path

The philosopher's stone embodies the hope that is at the heart of the hero's journey. Our assumption is that despite the chaos and complexity that typify much of education today, transformation is not only possible but inevitable. This reality is powerfully reflected in the New Science phenomenon of strange attractors. As described by Gleick, Wheatley, and others, these are archetypal basins of attraction that define and give ultimate form to what may appear, at times, as chaos and anarchy. In what subatomic physicists call "phase space," we discover that seemingly random and chaotic elements ultimately find some outlying structure and order that superimposes stability on a seemingly out-of-control system.

For educators entangled in the complex web of forces influencing school transformation, this view of order can be taken as a message of hope. If we believe that the most powerful learning occurs on the edge of chaos, then we view disorder, unpredictability, and confusion with a different mindset. We realize that, in the midst of what appears to be random capriciousness and loss of control, we may be moving to the discovery of a new order and a higher-level synthesis—the manifestation of all the potential inherent in the philosopher's stone. When we undertake the hero's journey with integrity, respect for others, and recognition of the interdependence of all of life, no matter how dark our circumstances may appear at the moment, the chaos and complexity we experience are prerequisite to the creation of new knowledge. As Gleick (1987) describes what he calls "The Geometry of Nature":

> Our feeling for beauty is inspired by the harmonious arrangement of order and disorder as it occurs in natural objects—in clouds, trees, mountain ranges, or snow crystals. The shapes of

all these are dynamical processes jelled into physical forms, and particular combinations of order and disorder are typical for them. (p. 117)

The phenomena of the New Science parallel the elements inherent in the mythic hero's journey, as well as the complex, multifaceted experiences of educators today: In the face of complacency, chaos, complexity, and an unpredictable future, there is an innate search for equilibrium, homeostasis, order, and peace—existential conditions that we can achieve if we are willing to undertake the quest. At its deepest level, our quest is to become fully self-aware as individuals and as systems. What was once unconscious and in control of us (the sprites and tricksters of mythic lore) become transformed into helpmates—or are dissolved into our own beings as some greater strength, power, and identity.

In mythology, the ultimate quest is to bring all the divided and disparate parts of the hero's personality into a harmonious and unifying whole. The result is a deeper level of self-knowledge, a higher degree of personal mastery, and a new level of consciousness. Because organizations possess all the characteristics of living systems, we believe that, as living entities, they are on a similar quest. On one level, there is dysfunction, fragmentation, discord, and conflicting ideas about vision and purpose and their translation to action. On another level, there is a quest for order, wholeness, and alignment. As Wheatley and Kellner-Rogers (1996) note in *A Simpler Way:*

> Organizations are living systems . . . [and] life self-organizes. Networks, patterns, and structures emerge without external imposition or direction. Organization wants to happen. (p. 3)

Finally, the New Science provides startling and powerful alternatives to the paradigm that undergirds much of educational theory and research (see Figure 2.1). As Stacey, Wheatley, Senge, and others suggest, the linear, clockwork Newtonian model of the universe—suggesting that all phenomena can somehow be categorized, analyzed, understood, and controlled using traditional scientific methods—has been replaced by a nonlinear, open-ended world of fractals, morphogenic field theory, and strange attractors. These concepts call into question many of the traditional expectations inherent in prequantum,

---

Figure 2.1
Two Paradigms

Newtonian Paradigm	New Science Paradigm
• Information as discrete bits. Parts-to-whole approach. • Nature as controllable and tamable. Cause and effect are closely related in time and space. • Learning as a stimulus-response process. • Clockwork universe as key metaphor.	• Information as primary connecting force. • We are partners with, not masters of, nature. Cause and effect often not easily analyzed or predicted. • Learning as a nonlinear, dialogical process of making meaning. • Quantum universe as key metaphor.

---

pre-New Science thinking. As we shall demonstrate later, when these new findings are applied to complex organizations (like schools and their systems), the implications are profound for such "tried and true" practices as: strategic planning, analytic problem solving, quantitative data collection and analysis, vision building, and a sequential, one-size-fits-all approach to teaching and learning.

Educational Change and the Process of Organizational Renewal for the Next Millennium

Although the Newtonian paradigm seems to be hanging on by its fingertips in scientific circles, it continues to dominate the thinking and operations of schools and school systems. At the same time, a complementary body of organizational literature is emerging that presents powerful and compelling conceptual maps—or philosopher's stones—for the hero's journey at the building and system level. The new gurus of organizational renewal suggest that the Newtonian model of the universe—based on a linear view of reality that assumes a predictable sequence between cause and effect—can no longer be the conceptual framework for creating successful organizations, such

as corporations, schools, or school systems. The organizational renewal literature suggests to us that the path of the hero's journey in
any arena, but particularly one as complex as the world of education,
requires attention to the unpredictable, nonlinear, and evolutionary
process of planning for change.

Citing the New Science paradigm, many theorists of the change
process in organizations (e.g., Senge, Fullan, Stacey, Wheatley) embrace the notion of a quantum universe, one characterized by paradox, patterns of simultaneous connection and dissolution, holism,
systems thinking, and relationship as the key determiners of what is
observed. Fullan (1993a) notes:

> Dynamic complexity is the real territory of change, when
> cause and effect are not close in time and space and obvious
> interventions do not produce expected outcomes. . . . We keep
> discovering as Dorothy in Oz did, that "I have a feeling we are
> not in Kansas anymore." Complexity, dynamism, and unpre-
> dictability, in other words are not merely things that get in the
> way. They are normal! (p. 20)

The emerging body of organizational renewal literature is not
without its perils. Its conceptual frameworks and operating principles
require a kind of steadfast determination to navigate the waters of oc-
casionally murky language, paradoxical recommendations, and contradictory declarations—not unlike the complexity and occasional
turmoil experienced by the mythic Odysseus, Dorothy, and Bilbo Baggins. For heroes embarking on their journeys, the road toward renewal and transformation is never entirely clear and certainly never
easy. What, then, can change theorists teach us about the heroic
school and the heroic school system? Wheatley (1992) provides a
wonderful starting point:

> My growing sensibility of a quantum universe has affected my
> organizational life in several ways. First, I try hard to discipline
> myself to remain aware of the whole and to resist my well-
> trained desire to analyze the parts to death. I look now for
> patterns of movement over time and focus on qualities like
> rhythm, flow, direction, and shape. Second, I know I am

wasting time whenever I draw straight arrows between two variables in a cause and effect diagram, or position things as polarities, or create elaborate plans and time lines. Third, I no longer argue with anyone about what is real. Fourth, the time I formerly spent on detailed planning and analysis I now use to look at the structures that might facilitate relationships. I have come to expect that something useful occurs if I link up people, units, or tasks, even though I cannot determine precise outcomes. And last, I realize more and more that the universe will not cooperate with my desires for determinism. (p. 43)

Like the animate landscapes and venues that shape the adventures of the mythic hero, organizations as described in the new leadership literature are conscious entities *with all the characteristics of a living system.* They have personalities, values, patterns of interaction, structures, internal processes, and self-referencing pathways. As Wheatley and Kellner-Rogers (1996, p. 58) suggest: "Every organization is an identity in motion, moving through the world, trying to make a difference."

Applying the New Cognitive and Brain Research to Individual and Organizational Learning

A fundamental tenet of our philosopher's stone is that both the mythic hero and the heroic educator learn through experience. The power of all great mythic tales is their reinforcement of this experience-based learning process. As readers, listeners, and viewers, we grow to learn about ourselves by witnessing the hero's struggle toward transformation. Like Odysseus, Dorothy, or Luke Skywalker, we discover that insight and understanding are impossible if we limit our learning to the study of someone else's knowledge. And as all mythic heroes learn, true education is self-education. Although mentors can guide us and colleagues can share what works for them, ultimately we walk the heroic path toward true awareness and insight alone. The true mentors and wisdom figures of world mythology—from Merlyn in *The Once and Future King* to Yoda in *Star Wars* to Maria in Bolman and Deal's (1995) allegory *Leading with Soul*—tend to ask questions rather than provide answers. Learning occurs in the hero's journey, as *The Wizard of Oz* reminds us, through the merging of head, heart, and courage.

Despite what we now know about the complexity of human learning at the individual and collective level, the behavioral-rational model that springs from the tradition of Skinner, Tyler, and Mager continues to dominate our thinking in education. This paradigm suggests that learning is neat, controllable, and programmable. It is grounded in empirical, behavioral notions of human learning, especially the idea that there is a discrete cause-effect linkage between teacher input and student output. In contrast, the New Science, particularly chaos and complexity theory, reinforces current constructivist and brain-based models that suggest that learning is open-ended, elliptical, recursive, and heavily influenced by context and the learner's cognitive schema.

The old paradigm of the factorylike, assembly line school typically ascribes to the notions that teaching is a "one-size-fits-all" process in which students are passive recipients of information dispensed by experts. In the heroic school and school system, educators view learning, instead, as relational, open-ended, and dependent on the teacher's ability to help a diverse group of students construct and experience meaning. This principle is essential to our philosopher's stone. As part of the hero's journey in education, it is insufficient for schools to mandate standards in which a body of declarative knowledge is dispensed and parroted back by students to demonstrate that they are educated. Instead, the heroic school and school system emphasize that information becomes knowledge only when students use it in meaningful ways. Heroic educators have the ability and commitment to make the boundaries between school and life fluid and permeable.

Emotion, the Learning Process, and the Hero's Journey

Essential to our notion of the philosopher's stone is the need for the heroic educator, school, and system to recognize that emotion, feeling, relationship, and human interaction all influence learning. Part of the vision quest in education is to rid ourselves of the illusion that emotion and cognition are separate entities—or that we can find one size of teaching to fit all learners. As the 1997 ASCD Yearbook, *Rethinking Educational Change with Heart and Mind*, affirms:

> If our attempts to go *wider* in our change efforts are to be educationally productive . . . we must also go *deeper* and examine

the moral grounds and emotional texture of our practice, of what it means to be a teacher. Our change priorities fail to develop what Goleman (1995) calls the emotional intelligence of students and teachers alike: emotional intelligence that actually adds value to students' classroom learning and teachers' professional learning. Educational change needs more depth. We need to put the heart back into it. Once we grasp this point of how to go deeper, we can then go wider in our change efforts beyond the school in ways that are purposeful and emotionally engaged, rather than through means that are opportunistic or bureaucratically superficial. (Hargreaves, 1997, p. 12)

On this level, the educational journey is also fraught with paradox. Here are some examples:

• The learner's search for involvement and meaning, extending from exciting educational experiences—juxtaposed against the barrenness that is often present in classrooms built on the industrial model of schooling.

• The tug of war between the relational and interactive nature of great learning—and the separation and isolation that are typical of many educational settings.

• The cohesiveness that extends from integrated and relevant learning activities—competing with the fragmentation associated with curriculum that is presented atomistically and didactically.

• The purposeful construction of personal and collective meaning sparked by the search for imaginative answers to compelling questions—contrasted with the boredom that occurs when instruction is presented as dogma.

• The sense of empowerment and efficacy students can experience in heroic classrooms—contrasted with the alienation and fragmentation students experience in industrial-model schools.

The enormous progress being made in modern cognitive theory and recent brain research confirms the vital link between emotions and learning. All great heroes ultimately learn that the intellect and the heart must be aligned if genuine transformation is to occur. This is another essential tenet of our philosopher's stone.

New Views of Learning

The hero's journey in education today requires that educators investigate, evaluate, and internalize the best of what we now know about the learning process. First, researchers in the areas of cognitive psychology, brain-compatible learning, and multiple intelligences are recognizing that learning is as complex and diverse as the human species. Most agree that the behaviorist model of learning is incomplete: We cannot teach everyone in the same way. Nor can higher-level thinking and learning occur in an environment of reward and punishment. We now know that cognition is not separate from emotion, and that learning occurs best in an atmosphere of high challenge and low threat. Teachers must attend to students' emotional and social needs by creating a classroom where trust, acceptance, respect, and caring are norms. As part of our philosopher's stone, we suggest the following principles of learning for the heroic school and school system:

1. *True learning comes from a fusion of head, heart, and body.* The knowledge and understanding that become a true part of ourselves are always the result of experiential learning in which we are intellectually connected, emotionally engaged, and physically involved. The heroic school and school system are places in which the joy and chaos of exploration and inquiry are dominant and always present.

2. *Learning occurs in heroic environments in which motivation is largely intrinsic rather than extrinsic.* In such an environment, all members of a school or school system are part of a genuine learning community. As Wheatley (1992, p. 12) suggests:

> We are refocusing on the deep longings we have for community, meaning, dignity, and love in our organizational lives. We are beginning to look at the strong emotions that are part of being human, rather than segmenting ourselves or believing that we can confine workers [students] into narrow roles, as though they were cogs in the machinery of production. As we let go of the machine models of work [and education], we begin to step back and see ourselves in new ways, to appreciate our wholeness, and to design organizations that honor and make use of the totality of who we are.

3. *The heroic school and school systems are brain-compatible learning environments.* Acknowledging that the brain is a pattern-seeking, meaning-making organ, such schools and systems plan curriculum, instruction, and assessment that are integrated and that stimulate students' diverse ways of knowing. They acknowledge that every learner's brain, as Renate and Geoffrey Caine (1991) remind us in *Making Connections*, is a uniquely organized system that is highly social and highly idiosyncratic. The search for meaning among all learners is innate and occurs through the continuing search by the brain for patterns and relevance to the learner. Heroic schools also recognize that emotions are a fundamental part of learning because the brain "downshifts" whenever there is a perceived threat or emotional upset, diminishing its capacity for engaging in higher-level thinking.

4. *The heroic school and system attend to the new findings in cognitive psychology and constructivist education.* They structure the learning process on the principle that knowledge is constructed—that learning is a process of creating personal meaning from new information by tying it to prior knowledge and experience. Like the hero's journey, learning is not linear; rather, it is recursive, iterative, and tied to particular situations. Students are unlikely to transfer information from one context to another unless their teachers offer them experiences that provide bridges, or scaffolds, to higher levels.

5. *Above all, learning is strategic.* It is goal oriented and involves the learner's assimilation of strategies associated with knowing when to use knowledge, how to adapt it, and how to manage one's own learning process (Herman, Aschbacher, & Winters, 1992; Marzano, 1992).

The Power of Myth and Metaphor

The final element of our philosopher's stone is the recognition that myth and metaphor can be powerful devices for deepening our understanding and knowledge of complex phenomena. They enable us to build bridges between the known and the unknown through in-depth comparisons. In this sense, metaphors function in a variety of ways: as insights, as discoveries, as arguments, as mental models, and as theories (Pugh, 1989). As Howard Peelle suggests:

> Metaphors cultivate the mind. They prepare furrows for plant-
> ing ideas, which in time grow to mature understanding. If the
> climate is too arid for learning or if work as been neglected for
> too long, metaphors can break through an unreceptive crust to
> more fertile ground where the nutrients of teaching and under-
> standing can be absorbed. (cited in Pugh, 1989, p. 19)

Through metaphorical thinking, meanings become unified and integrated into the underlying patterns that constitute our conceptual
understanding of reality. Through metaphor we extend our understanding of the connection of one phenomenon to another. If there is
a clear fit, we know that this understanding is structural and relational,
not confined to any particular item or concept (Pugh, 1989). In *The
Creative Brain*, Herrmann (1988) suggests that metaphors can bridge
cultures, languages, and brain-dominance preferences. As a product
of the right brain, notes Herrmann, a metaphor can be thought of as a
translation from one mental language to another, from the literal to the
analogous. Its power is the instant understanding that it brings by reason of the translation.

The metaphor of the hero's journey, then, can provide us in education with a shared set of symbols through which to describe the patterns and lived experiences that unite us, even in times of difficulty
and transition. In exploring the parallels between the lives of the great
mythic heroes and their progress toward insight and transformation,
we can find analogies to describe our individual and collective movement as educators from innocence and denial to chaos and complexity and, ultimately, to revelation. We can learn at least one set of
metaphorical pathways toward individual renewal and organizational
empowerment.

Myths and Metaphors as Bridges Between the Known and Unknown

In "Metaphors and Multiples," Maxine Greene (1997) notes:

> A metaphor enables us to understand one thing better by lik-
> ening it to what it is not. . . . A metaphor not only involves a re-
> orientation of consciousness; it also enables us to cross
> divides, to make connections between ourselves and others,
> and to look through other eyes. . . . For Hannah Arendt, the
> metaphor of "bridging the abyss between inward and invisible

mental activities and the world of appearances" was certainly the greatest gift language could bestow on thinking. (p. 391)

In a quantum universe and an age of rising complexity, myth and metaphor can provide us with collective symbols and icons for describing unconscious experiences in education, as well as emerging insights. When we find ourselves threatened by the enormity of the change process, for example, we can remind ourselves of the inevitable fears and anxieties experienced by all mythic heroes on the road to transformation.

Similarly, when we find ourselves isolated and despondent about the failure of a particular innovation or program, we can recollect the ways in which mythic heroes found strength in wisdom figures and companions along the way who assisted them in rejoining the splintered parts of themselves. And when we find ourselves experiencing triumphs and breakthroughs, we can recall the inevitable need to celebrate and engage in acknowledgment rituals, as we see in virtually every great mythic tradition and classic of mythic literature. These myths and metaphors can serve as guidemaps to inform our collective journey toward the unknown.

Myths and Metaphors as Mental Models That Shape Action

In our struggle to construct meaning in our lives, we frequently miss the fact that the metaphors we use become our mental models. As such, they not only shape the way we see the world, but they also influence the decisions we make—or don't make—and the actions we take—or don't take. In a recent article in the *Phi Delta Kappan* (May 1997), Peel and McCary argue that the "new metaphor for schooling" adopted by their district has enabled them to devise a "more powerful vision for schooling" on which they now plan to act. Similarly, in *Education Week,* Kohn (1997) argues that "our use of workplace metaphors may compromise the essence of schooling":

Importing the nomenclature of the workplace is something most of us do without thinking—which in itself is a good reason to reflect on the practice. Every time we talk about "homework" or "seat work" or "work habits" . . . we are using a metaphor with profound implications for the nature of schooling. In effect, we are equating what children do in school to figure things out [and make meaning of the world] with what adults do in offices and factories to earn money. (p. 60)

The metaphor and myth of the hero's journey can serve as a powerful frame or mental model to guide and inform the process of educational transformation. The mythic hero, in effect, can become a personification of the recursive and inevitable transitions that the individual, the school, and the school system must experience as they work to make education authentic, purposeful, and resonant for contemporary students. Each of us, for example, experiences at one time or another the longing or nostalgia for some distant past representing a missing piece of ourselves and our world, just as every mythic hero does at some point. Similarly, most educators, school-based staff members, and school system employees have at times experienced the sense that they are in combat with opposing forces that lead them through trials, tests, and initiations.

Myths and Metaphors as Problem-Solving Tools

Beyond shaping the way we think and act, metaphors also help us to solve problems. As Barell (1991) suggests in *Teaching for Thoughtfulness*: "Metaphors help us frame dilemmas in such a way that solutions appear" (p. 177). In *Teaching for the Two-Sided Mind*, Linda Williams (1983) tells the story of Charles Duryea, an engineer who had been struggling with the apparently unsolvable problem of how to develop an efficient system for introducing fuel into the engine of an automobile:

One day in 1891 he observed his wife at her dressing table spraying herself with her perfume atomizer. Although Duryea knew about the function and existence of perfume atomizers, he had not made a connection until that moment; but now he saw at once how to build the spray-injection carburetor. (p. 27)

The mythic journeys of the great hero figures parallel this problem-solving process. Each of the archetypal hero figures we encounter in literature—from Bilbo Baggins to Black Elk to Dante, Odysseus, and Dorothy—personify the stages of metaphorical thinking and problem solving. They begin in a problem-solving mode in which they experience, process, and keep redefining the central problem(s) they encounter. Their initial insights come as a result of their meetings with external "wisdom figures." As the hero's journey progresses, however, this externalized knowledge becomes internalized and assimilated into the hero's own way of viewing the world.

Making the Strange Familiar

Von Oech (1983) notes that metaphors are quite effective at making complex ideas easier to understand. They can be good tools to use for explaining complex ideas to people outside their own areas of expertise. He uses the example of explaining Dolby sound in nontechnical terms:

> Dolby is like sonic laundry. It washes out the dirt (noise) out of clothes (the signal) without disturbing the clothes (the signal).

In effect, this entire book is an attempt to make the strange familiar within the world of education. By examining the phases of the hero's journey and its parallels to our collective journey in schools and school systems today, we can distance ourselves from the immediacy of our day-to-day struggles and superimpose on our lives a powerful and dramatic new set of lenses through which we view our world. We become Black Elk confronting the unity of the cosmos and the interconnectedness of physical phenomena. We become Arjuna finding moral and spiritual purpose in the face of discord and alienation. We become Odysseus and Dorothy, finding our way back to the security of our homeland, but making the voyage with a renewed sense of insight and wisdom. We become Luke Skywalker finding the physical strength and internal resolve to overcome the "dark side of the Force." And we become the great explorers of the underworld—from Dante to Bilbo Baggins—finding a way out to the light when darkness seems to be enfolding us.

As educators embarking on this journey, we have the opportunity to grow and change—but more significantly, we have the opportunity to help transform the kingdom of education. Joseph Campbell (1949) emphasizes that the hero is a "champion not of things become but of things becoming; the dragon to be slain by him is precisely the monster of the status quo: Holdfast the keeper of the past." The hero's task

---

Figure 2.2
Six Phases of the Hero's Journey

1. Innocence Lost

2. Chaos and Complexity

3. The Heroic Quest

4. Gurus and Alliances

5. Trials, Tests, and Initiations

6. Insight and Transformation

---

has always been to bring new life to a dying culture (Campbell & Moyers, 1988).

Although the distinctions among the major phases of the hero's evolution are recursive and intricately interconnected, we have identified six structural divisions of the journey (Figure 2.2). Each division helps define the roadmap for the journey; but like the phenomena they describe, they should be considered metaphors themselves, rather than absolutes. Finally, each of these phases is guided and informed by a series of essential questions. We have framed these questions as "Reflection Checkpoints" in each of the subsequent chapters.

Our hope is that this roadmap will enhance educators' understanding of the ambitious and daunting process they are undertaking in collaborating to transform education today. Pandit Rajmani Tigunait summarizes the power of this metaphorical excursion in his work *Inner Quest* (1995):

> The heroic quest is often spoken of as a journey. And any journey, whether in the realm of geography or in the realm of the spirit, proceeds in stages. If you live in Colorado, for instance, you cannot trek to a hidden valley in the Himalayas until you have found your way to an airport, flown to Asia, and hired a vehicle to convey you into the mountains. If you are smart, you will have talked to people who have made similar treks, located your route on a map, purchased a reliable guidebook, and spent some time hiking in the Rockies, acclimating your

body and breath to high-altitude exertion. The hero's journey is no different: to reach your goal you need some idea of the terrain that lies between you and your destination and a plan for crossing it. Like any traveler, you will want an accurate map, the best information you can get from those who have made the trip before you, and a reliable guidebook if one is to be had. (pp. xi–xii)

3

INNOCENCE LOST

BREAKDOWN REQUIRES BREAKTHROUGH

━━━━━━━━━

> Don't turn from the delight
> that is so close at hand!
> Don't find some lame excuse
> to leave our gathering.
> You were a lonely grape
> and now you are sweet wine.
> There is no use in trying to
> become a grape again.
>
> —JALALUDDIN RUMI, 13th century Sufi poet,
> *IN THE ARMS OF THE BELOVED* (1997)

Every heroic journey begins with its hero or heroine in a state of unconscious innocence. It parallels the Sufi poet Rumi's metaphor for human beings' attempts to recapture what once was but now has passed away, or as he puts it: "There is no use in [wine] trying to become a grape again." For Joseph Campbell, this condition is the precursor to the "Call to Adventure" and the "Road of Trials," the great archetypal signals that the hero's journey has begun. Mythic figures—like heroic educators, schools, and systems—are in an initial state of innocence whenever they display an unconscious naivete about themselves, the complexity of the world they inhabit, or the difficulty of the road awaiting them.

❖ ❖ ❖

When Telemachus, son of the great Greek warrior Odysseus, struggles at the beginning of *The Odyssey* to fend off his mother's unwanted suitors, he exists in a condition of untested innocence in which his potential as a great leader remains hidden and suppressed. At the beginning of the epic, we meet him in a condition of despair and confusion, which eventually disappear only when he willingly accepts the destiny awaiting him. He assumes his rightful mantle as the heir to Odysseus when he ceases his self-doubt and self-imposed constraints and opens himself to the world, not just the restricted shelter of his life in Ithaca.

Similarly, when Dorothy in *The Wizard of Oz* struggles valiantly to return to her Kansas homeland, she remains in a state of innocence so long as she assumes that something or someone outside herself can bring her home again. It is only when she uncovers the strength of character that is her birthright that she unlocks the door that separates her from her Kansas farm and family. In moving through that door, she gains a transforming strength and a wisdom that she would have lost had she not been forced to take her journey through the wonderland of Oz.

The condition of unconscious innocence also manifests itself in *Star Wars* whenever Luke Skywalker clings to the less evolved parts of his character, either denying or not using his innate gifts as a potential Jedi knight. For Luke, this condition of innocence remains as long as his potential lies fallow and unchallenged. It diminishes and ultimately disappears when he confronts the dark sides of his own character and purifies them through overcoming the tests he confronts on his quest to restore freedom to the galaxy.

❖ ❖ ❖

Innocence is a condition that we as educators experience whenever we long for simpler times or think we can return to the past. Like all great mythic heroes, we cease to grow if we remain in this state of unconsciousness and denial. The state of innocence endures as long as we believe that individuals or forces outside ourselves can provide easy solutions to the complex and, at times, chaotic problems that confront us today. A nationally recognized principal we interviewed on this issue suggested:

> Innocence for me shows up in educators' wishing for the good old days, the way it was when we went to school. I hear about that a great deal . . . a wishing that the "old" population who really loved school—those kids who came ready and those immigrant people who knew the real value of education—would return. It is a belief that if we could get that back, we could do remarkable things.

For educators, this state of unconscious innocence can take the form of faculty room reminiscences about "the way kids used to be" and "remember when _____ was principal?" It is also present whenever we are tempted to close our classroom doors and remain in a state of separation, preferring to do "our own thing" rather than working with others to forge a more powerful and vision-driven future. Similarly, for school-based administrators, innocence may show up as a fondness for times when everyday life in schools seemed less riddled by crisis and turmoil—when mandates and policies seemed enough to bring order out of complexity (see Figure 3.1).

Figure 3.1
Innocence Lost and the Call to Action

All great mythic quests and journeys represent movements away from the stability, comfort, and safety of the known in response to external opportunities or threats. In school communities, innocence might be characterized by the following:

- Nostalgia for the past.
- If only . . .
- This too shall pass.
- Outworn paradigms or mindsets.
- The belief in silver bullets or one-size-fits-all.
- The "experts" have the answers.

For superintendents, it can take the form of a wistful longing for a not-too-long-ago era when Boards of Education seemed more laissez-faire and less policitized and constituent-driven. Innocence at this level is present whenever policies, bulletins, and declarations replace dialogue and consensus-driven problem solving and decision making involving all relevant stakeholders. For parents, unconscious innocence is a pervasive nostalgia for simpler times, a fondness for recollecting perceived order, stability, and standards related to a past that may have existed—or may never have existed in any physical locale. Inevitably, we know that innocence is present whenever anyone blames schools and school systems for not *"being the way they used to be."*

The "Innocence Lost" phase of the educational hero's journey stems from a sense that a breakdown has occurred—or is about to. Although this breakdown requires powerful and immediate action, the chaos and complexity of the times often preclude the individual's or group's ability to react. Ultimately, the hero's journey in education—the path away from unconscious innocence toward enlightened engagement—involves taking a path of direct experience in which we confront change issues head-on. The same urban principal cited previously also emphasized:

> The state of innocence for educators and the public is the desire to return to the "good old days." It takes the form of statements like: "If we could just go back to the basics, we'd be fine." In fact, there were no good old days. *These* are the good old days right now. And the only use of the memory of the good old days is to help us reflect on the question: What did we do then that worked that needs to be transported to the present? What are the things we didn't do that we ought to have done? We need to amalgamate everything we know—past practices, current research, and everything useful in between—so that all children can learn.

Innocence Lost and the Heroic Educator

Educators, schools, and school systems today are struggling to regain a sense of shared assumptions and consensus-driven beliefs in the face of the chimera of change. The overwhelming psychological, social, economic, and technological forces confronting us these days can throw us all into a feeling of complexity bordering on chaos. Although we may be unconscious about it, we are all experiencing our lives in education today in a quantum state: We sense that we are locked in a series of dissipative structures that, quantum physicists tell us, appear to lapse into randomness before they reformulate themselves into a new structural identity. Like the phenomenon of strange attractors within the world of subatomic particles, we are caught in a seeming whirligig of capricious change that we think ought to lead to a set of defining parameters—but frequently appears not to do so.

The sense of spinning out of control that typifies many of our experiences in education is often accompanied by our inclination to revert back to the sense of a lost past. We are nostalgic for a lost set of values, shared beliefs, and standards that we dimly believe we once had in common—but have now, somehow, lost. At the beginning of our hero's journey in education, we find ourselves in a Tower of Babel of our own unconscious creation. We lack a common language, a common set of operating principles that shape and inform our behavior and actions. Heroic educators beginning their journey uncover this condition of unconscious innocence when they can recognize some of the following patterns in their professional lives and the lives of colleagues:

1. *The belief that "this too shall pass":* We may unconsciously assume that all educational changes are essentially temporal and subject to extinction. In effect, we believe that if we just wait long enough, this new issue or initiative will go away, just like every other innovation we've tried. This belief is evident in many ways, such as staff resistance to standards and accountability; teachers' hesitancy to adopt new instructional methods (e.g., cooperative learning); and administrators' discomfort with relinquishing control when school-based management is introduced.

2. *The assumption that it's enough "just to care about the kids":* We may hold the well-intentioned but naive presumption that our concern and dedication are sufficient to ensure that the school in which we work is a true learning organization. If we just care about kids, we may argue, everything else will take care of itself. This assumption is evident when well-intentioned teachers fail to acknowledge the growing knowledge base on teaching strategies that are directly tied to gains in student achievement.

3. *The perception that everyone shares common values and beliefs about education:* This pattern is a variation of the second one. It involves an untested assumption that everyone both feels and thinks alike about the purpose of education and about the welfare of the students we serve. This misperception can and does lead to confusion and disappointment whenever educational change is involved. This perception is particularly troublesome in light of the increasingly diverse, multicultural student populations that schools today serve. Like all heroic mythic patterns, what is unconscious and untested will inevitably result in trials, tests, and challenges that will separate baser metals from gold.

4. *The assumption that "we all speak the same language":* As educators, many of us have the recurrent misperception that we are all using terms, concepts, and generalizations in the same way. Holding on to this assumption weakens staff members' ability to take advantage of the full power of strategic school improvement planning. When staff fail to recognize the value of building common agreement about values, norms, and standards, they lose the opportunity to move from isolation to schoolwide action toward common goals. The willingness to achieve consensus about what the language of change means operationally is a critical indicator that the heroic educator is moving from innocence onto the path of the hero's journey.

5. *Untested or unchallenged "if only" thinking:* One of the great pitfalls facing us is the very human tendency to lapse into dichotomous and simplistic thinking. Here are two examples: "If only I had better students" or "If only the administration and central office really understood what we are dealing with in our classrooms."

6. *The belief that the educator's lot in life is one of isolation and separation:* The 19th century model of schooling that still pervades our thinking in education is at the heart of our unconscious perceptions. Essentially, factory models of schools reinforce the notion that we are "all in this alone." We are conditioned to believe that the power of the teacher working alone is greater than the amassed synergy of shared decision making, planning, and problem solving.

What, then, can the mythic hero's journey teach us about dealing with the condition of Innocence Lost at the individual or personal level? In many of the great world mythologies, this initial state of innocence is triggered by a confrontation with some powerful change force that triggers an internal drive to discover who we are and where we fit into the cosmic scheme. Although this struggle to know ourselves is as archetypal and deeply rooted in the human experience as any other innate drive, it can simultaneously trigger a desire to retreat from the journey and become paralyzed with anxiety about the change process.

❖ ❖ ❖

Arjuna, for example, is the human protagonist of the great Indian spiritual classic, *The Bhagavad Gita* (trans. Sri Swami Satchidananda, 1997). Seated in his chariot, Arjuna is a powerful warrior about to engage in battle, when he sees his own kinsmen and his revered teacher arrayed in battle against him. Confronting this new version of a past that was once comforting to him, he feels immobilized; he cannot fight. It is then that Krishna, the Lord of the Cosmos, comes to counsel him. Overcome with sentimentality and momentary loss of a sense of duty, Arjuna experiences shivering and dryness of throat, nearly fainting from despondency. He lacks the language, the conceptual and emotional apparatus, to open himself to the experience he is facing. Deciding not to fight, he longs for earlier times and pleads to Krishna:

> I am weighed down with weakmindedness; I am confused and cannot understand my duty. I beg of you to say for sure what is right for me to do. I am your disciple. Please teach me, for I have taken refuge in you. (p. 11)

Our contemporary world of film is also full of images of the innocence experience that begins the hero's journey. Luke Skywalker in *Star Wars,* for example, is not unlike Arjuna at the beginning of the *Gita.* When we first meet him, Luke is riddled with doubt and frustration about his own destiny. He lacks the conceptual language to describe his longing to become a Jedi warrior, feeling powerless to persuade his uncle and aunt that he has some greater destiny than the one they are imposing on him. Mired down by responsibility for his family and tasks on his home planet of Tatooin, Luke feels a terrible world weariness, an innate longing for experience and purpose that his arid, stagnant life as a farmer fails to provide him. It is only when destiny intervenes, in the form of a three-foot metal droid with a holographic cry for help from a desperate princess, that Luke begins to assert himself and respond to his calling. When starship troopers destroy his adopted home, his fate is sealed, his innocence is lost, and his hero's journey begins.

❖ ❖ ❖

In education today, the heroic educator's stage of innocence can take the form of naive assumptions that the educational vocabulary we use means the same thing to everyone. We may fail to question often enough the extent to which we substantively understand what we are saying to one another about the teaching and learning process—and its outcomes. We frequently work at cross purposes because members of the school and its community do not share a common language about what precisely constitutes quality instruction. Our innocence extends, in part, from a collective failure to develop a consensus-based vision and common standards and values about the purpose and outcomes of education. At the outset, when confronting the complexities of situations in which we lack operational language and shared values, resistance is a natural response to transition and an inevitable part of the change process (Bridges, 1991; Fullan & Miles, 1992; Maurer, 1996). See Chapter 7 for a discussion of responding to resistance to change.

The individual educators we interviewed consistently reflected these patterns and motifs in their description of the experience of innocence and innocence lost in the world of education. One district administrator, for example, described her experience of confronting the limitations of unconscious innocence in this way:

> I lost my innocence when I realized that there were a lot of decisions being made that were not about what is good for the kids. People were not stopping to ask: How will this decision affect teachers in the classroom? How will it affect children in the schools?"

Another administrator reflected the same feelings:

From the time I was in the classroom—and that was many years—I always believed that we made decisions that were best for the kids. The further away I moved from the classroom, the more I began to see that this wasn't the case. When I moved out of the classroom, it broke my bubble.

This archetypal condition of "awakening" is the inevitable catalyst for the heroic educator to move from innocence onto the road of the heroic journey. For the people we interviewed, perhaps the most profound manifestation of this phenomenon resulted when they combined their experiences as professional educators with their heartfelt experiences as parents. One such educator, who has spent her professional life working in a variety of parent and community outreach programs, described her awakening from innocence this way:

I think I began to lose my innocence when my children first started going to school. Before my first child started, I really believed in public education, and that everyone really wanted what was best for children. And then reality hit on the first day of kindergarten. The first interaction I had with the school as a parent was cold, distant. As if they were saying: "You just leave your son with us. Parents don't come into school."

REFLECTION CHECKPOINT: The Heroic Educator

1. To what extent have I demonstrated a belief that "this too shall pass"? Have I contributed to my school's organizational culture by adding cynicism or skepticism to the process of reform?

2. How have I made an effort to express and share my values about education and the learning process with my colleagues?

3. To what extent can I articulate values that I share in common with my coworkers?

4. To what extent can I articulate areas where my values about education and learning differ significantly from the individuals with whom I work?

5. To what extent do I avoid "if only" thinking?

6. How have I contributed to overcoming professional isolation and separation within my classroom, grade level, or department?

Innocence Lost and the Heroic School

The hero's state of innocence can also take the form of longing for a return to some Golden Age, a Paradise Lost, a condition that is most characteristic of many schools before they undertake the journey. In the face of an overwhelming complexity bordering on chaos, schools often resist change and avoid the journey. As a collective unit, many schools elect instead—albeit unconsciously—to hold onto a condition of nostalgia for some idyllic past that appears to have been taken from them by circumstances beyond their control. We often hear the "if only" list from educators:

- "If only the kids had good homes."
- "If only we didn't have to deal with such diversity."
- "If only parents could read to their children at home."
- "If only kids respected authority (or each other)."
- "If only the district, school board, or state would stop bugging us."
- "If only we didn't have to cover the curriculum and teach to the test."

The litany goes on. In clinging to a past that is gone (or perhaps never *was*), we fail to look ahead to the possibilities and opportunities in both the present and the future.

❖ ❖ ❖

The tradition of great mythic literature is full of tensions between what *was* and what *may be*. In John G. Neihardt's life story of a Holy Man of the Oglala Sioux, *Black Elk Speaks* (1979), for example, the tension among the past, present, and future takes the form of a great vision revealed to the protagonist, Black Elk. A great shaman recounts to him a time in the earth's history when unity, order, and balance were omnipresent in the world, a time before the devastation of the Custer battle, the Ghost Dance, and the Wounded Knee massacre. Black Elk retains this vision of a unified and holistic universe when he confronts the great tragedies that will befall his people, including the virtual elimination of the physical environment that shaped and defined their culture. He returns to this great vision as a powerful iconic image of a unity that once existed, but is lost to the majority of beings now. Above all, he is struck by the relentless tension between the devastation and chaos that work to destroy the Sioux culture and the controlling spiritual principles that guide and inform the physical universe when humanity has the spiritual insight to recognize them.

Similarly, Dante in *The Divine Comedy* begins his journey through Hell, Purgatory, and Paradise with a declaration of a time lost, of how he strayed from the true path:

> In the middle of the journey of our life I came to myself within a dark wood where the straight way was lost. Ah, how hard a thing it is to tell of that wood, savage and harsh and dense, the thought of which renews my fear? But to give account of the good which I found there I will tell of the other things I noted there. (Dante, *Inferno,* 1961, p. 23)

Dante's description of the beginning of his journey echoes with the nostalgia and longing for a path and a time now lost to him, a condition precipitated by his descent into unconsciousness:

> I cannot rightly tell how I entered there, I was so full of sleep at that moment when I left the true way. . . . My mind, which was still in flight, turned back to look again at the path which never yet let any go alive. (p. 23)

❖ ❖ ❖

This sense of nostalgia and the pervasive desire to return to what we perceive as easier, safer times and locales typifies the staff of the heroic school during its innocence stage. In such a school, many staff members seem to have "rearview mirror thinking"; some see current change and complexity as both threatening and painful. Rather than confronting present realities head-on, they may prefer, instead, to retreat to the ease and placidity of what their consciousness suggests were better times. Often we call these individuals "resisters." But as Fullan and Miles (1992) emphasize:

> Any significant change involves a period of intense personal and organizational learning and problem solving. People need support for such work, not displays of impatience. (p. 748)

In effect, the innocence phase of the heroic school's journey emerges as a normal and predictable part of the process of both individuals' and groups' ability to construct personal meaning about the necessity or wisdom of changing behaviors, practices, values, and beliefs. For the school, the beginning of the heroic journey also involves confronting the conflicts and disconnects extending from differing visions, values, and operating principles. When the staff of the heroic school is in a state of innocence, they fail to recognize fully the extent to which their shared values may not, in fact, be shared at all. One of the principals we interviewed described this realization:

> Innocence was lost for me when I realized that people were not in education for the same reasons I was. They really weren't in education for education. There were other motives. And they didn't believe, as I did, that the child is the most important. Instead, it was the regulations or the politics or moving up the ladder or not making the person at the top angry that mattered most. I realized that no matter what you do, there is going to be a political element in it: advancement, control, and power, rather than looking at what the mission is and what we should be trying to accomplish with the kids.

What are the patterns of behavior within the heroic school that suggest that its staff are in a stage of unconscious innocence in their collective journey? Both the research associated with school renewal and interviews we conducted reflect the following parallel themes:

1. *The belief that values are either insignificant or do not need to be articulated:* In this first stage of the school's journey, teachers and administrators may not recognize that any organization, particularly an educational one, is essentially a collection of values and beliefs held by many different people. Before the journey toward meaningful school change begins, many members of the school community may be operating at cross purposes because of a failure to identify and collectively reinforce common values and beliefs about the learning and teaching process. Similarly, many teachers and administrators consistently hold the naive belief that articulating such values is unimportant.

2. *The assumption that anything involving change can be handled quickly, efficiently, and linearly:* When a school remains in a condition of unconscious innocence, its staff tends to operate in a naive state of disbelief and denial about the inevitable complexity and difficulty of effecting change in education. This disbelief and denial can lead to one-shot, inoculation-style staff development sessions (with accompanying notions that everyone should be "cured" as a result of this one-time intervention), as well as to management by mandate and fiat. When inevitable problems and blind alleys appear during the change process, staff members may be quick to place blame or give up on the initiative.

3. *The perception that "top-down" is always better than "bottom-up":* This perception surfaces during times of transition or high accountability. There is perhaps no more obvious time for it to surface than during times when testing and assessment are priorities. The school that has not yet fully committed to the heroic journey rarely allots the time and resources for bottom-up, collaborative decision making and problem solving. It tends to allow others to determine its agenda, and it allows itself to be controlled by top-down mandates. This passivity, in turn, reinforces a diminished sense of personal and professional efficacy and an organizational culture of bureaucratic control.

4. *The belief that we can either "tinker around the edges" or standardize chaos and complexity out of our school or district:* This common misperception is a hallmark of schools and districts in the stage of unconscious innocence. At one level, such schools and districts operate as if only small changes are needed to address the complex issues they face. School and district staff may discount the value of the research base on learning, school culture, job-embedded staff development, and collaborative school improvement planning. They tend toward one-size-fits-all thinking and away from individualizing practices to accommodate specific staff, student, or parental needs.

5. *The practice of not opening doors to parents and the community:* Out of unconscious innocence, many schools operate as a world unto themselves. Rather than taking advantage of the power and creativity that can be realized through parent and community

partnerships, such schools are castles with their drawbridges raised. This practice reflects two closely related mindsets: (a) We can do it better without help from the outside, and (b) we have enough to do already. Parents and community involvement will only complicate the issue.

6. *The belief that resistance is bad and change is good:* This type of either/or thinking represents an oversimplified view of the complexity involved in asking people, on a moment's notice, to change their practices, values, or beliefs. School staffs beginning their heroic journey need to reframe resistance as a natural response to transition. As in every great hero's journey, change involves loss: loss of the familiar, loss of ease with comfortable practices. Inevitably, accepting something new often means letting go of something old (Bridges, 1991). Unconsciously, we often characterize staff members' feelings of loss and vulnerability as "resistance to change." Proponents of educational change sometimes fail to understand that resistance is

---

REFLECTION CHECKPOINT: The Heroic School

1. In what ways are we unconscious about the issues and problems facing us?

2. To what extent do the climate, culture, and organization at our school reflect the belief that values are significant and that people should express them?

3. To what extent do our school improvement planning efforts take into account the complex, nonlinear nature of the change process?

4. To what extent do we avoid quick fixes and easy solutions to problems that are complex and multifaceted?

5. To what extent are shared decision making, problem solving, and inquiry a fundamental part of our school operations?

6. To what extent do we avoid the tendency to "tinker around the edges," with a consistent commitment to depth and clarity rather than breadth and quick completions of tasks and initiatives?

7. How have we helped parents and community members to become active and regular parts of our school improvement planning process?

often intended not to attack those advocating change, but to *protect* the resisters (Saxl, Miles, & Lieberman, 1990). Blaming resisters for the slow pace of reform keeps us from respecting individuals and groups and their need for time and support. People need time to assess educational change for its genuine possibilities and for how it bears on their values and self-interest (Fullan & Miles, 1992). Teachers and administrators need to listen to the concerns of "resisters" with respect.

Innocence Lost and the Heroic School System

All great mythic quests and journeys are movements away from the stability, comfort, and reassurance of the predictable and toward some future whose characteristics are hidden and seemingly unformed. Such a future is a bit like the *strange attractor* phenomenon described by quantum physicists: The outlying structure and order that will ultimately reveal themselves are not immediately apparent in the face of the chaos and complexity that pervade the field of subatomic particles. Ultimately, the hero's journey results in a more enlightened and holistic self-awareness on the part of the individual hero or heroine. These outcomes, however, can appear only if the mythic protagonists heed the call and move beyond the stability of the known. As one national administrator we interviewed described it:

> Innocence is tinkering around the edges . . . not facing reality. It comes from not realizing that we can't accomplish our educational goals within the "box" of the current system. The system as it is now structured does not support first-in-the-world teaching and learning. We need to be asking much harder questions, like: What is learning? Where is school?

Change in educational systems is a complex political, social, and personal process. In addition, the life cycle of educational innovations is relatively short. Because many systems do not accommodate staff members' need for ongoing support during a change process, schools frequently do not achieve the intended impact of innovations in teaching and learning. Thus, educators may frequently be skeptical or suspicious when a change appears on the horizon, fearing the start-up of another ill-conceived panacea—sometimes known as the "educational bandwagon" phenomenon.

At the system level, what are the patterns of behavior that suggest an organizational stage of innocence in the collective hero's journey? Once again, both the research associated with the school renewal process and the interviews we conducted reveal powerful complementary themes:

1. ***The belief in panaceas:*** A surefire way to identify a school system in a state of unconscious innocence is to find extensive evidence of leaders' attempts at quick fixes, one-shot interventions, and magic bullets. This phenomenon pervades much of educational reform today. Once again, it harkens back to the Industrial Age model of schooling that we seem to cling to. This pattern is present whenever a school system fails to take into account the need for involving all stakeholders in key systemic change initiatives. It shows up whenever leaders view any extended dialogue on purposes and meanings as luxuries that can be sacrificed for the sake of efficiency. Such "luxuries" include consensus building and attempts to achieve agreement on the meaning of terms (e.g., performance assessments, authentic assessment, standards, and benchmarks). A "quick fix" is in operation whenever school system leaders mandate quick, sweeping changes without providing the infrastructure, resources, and training to make the changes successful, organic parts of system operations.

2. ***The attitude that one size can fit all:*** Standardization of practice pervades many school systems today. Specifically, it takes the form of an inflexible commitment to standardization and bureaucratic control at the expense of practitioner input, involvement, and buy-in. In such a condition of innocence, we continue to hold on to outworn paradigms of educational structures (vestiges of an antiquated model of schools as factories). Increasingly, the change-dominated, technology-driven world of the 21st century looms before us. We must, as systems and as a profession, move beyond a one-size-fits-all mindset toward an organizational capacity for addressing students' and staff members' individual strengths and needs.

3. ***The perception that mandates and fiats are enough:*** Like the previous two conditions, school systems in a condition of unconscious innocence often operate from a belief in the power of mandate, declaration, and policy. Many educational leaders believe that "put-

ting it on paper" will be enough to ensure that an initiative, program, or priority will be implemented. This fundamental naivete fails completely to take into account how much school systems can thrive when norms of collegiality, interactivity, and dialogue exist. The only real and enduring changes within a system occur as a result of consensus building and shared inquiry. Although top-down visioning may work, top-down declarations can be ignored, misunderstood, and skillfully circumvented if key stakeholders remain out of the loop and ill informed.

4. *The belief that experts can save us:* In education, we live in a world of gurus and experts. As Canadian educator Barrie Bennett (personal interview, 1998) notes, however, gurus may proliferate, but we see little evidence in education of their individual contributions making much of a difference. "I wish," he told us, "that we would learn to internalize what these gurus have to say by putting their ideas into practice and learning from one another what works—and what doesn't." As Bennett suggests, no true change or transformation will occur within a system if its members cling to the outworn notion that some external expert—or set of experts—can ever save us. External knowledge remains just that: It can become wisdom and transformative in its impact only when teachers, administrators, and others in a school system construct meaning about that knowledge and make it their own through application and shared inquiry.

5. *The practice of adding to but never subtracting from:* As Art Costa once said, "Curriculum is like a cemetery. We keep putting things in, and never take anything out!" Costa's dictum—a frequent admonition in his speeches and presentations—has wide-ranging application to most systemic practices within education. Unconsciously innocent school systems do just what Costa suggests: They keep adding, but they never take anything away. The sense of *initiative overload* frequently leads school-based staffs to two almost inevitable conclusions: (a) The district office just doesn't understand what schools are asked to accomplish, and (b) the only logical thing to do is close the door and hope this stuff will go away. Obviously, part of the hero's journey for a school system is to minimize the effects of this cynicism by ensuring that school-based staffs play an active, purposeful, and ongoing role in key initiatives and programs. Planned obso-

lescence—the willingness of a school system to discard as well as add to—becomes a keystone of the heroic system moving away from innocence toward the heroic path.

As a system, how do we go beyond unconscious innocence and enter the road of the hero's journey? To equip ourselves for the journey, we may need to forsake antiquated notions of how learning occurs and how to structure and operate educational institutions. Like newcomers to a brave new world of quantum science and organizational transformation theory, we must accept that chaos, complexity, and discord are fundamental components of what's been called the "post-modern society," including the educational arena. The breakdowns requiring breakthroughs shaping our hero's journey in education today include our individual and collective tendency to deny the realities of the world we now inhabit, which education is responsible for serving.

If our schools and school systems are to become heroic, we must replace industrial models of administration and supervision—which result in nonproductive and inauthentic relationships among staff members and students—with more collegial, collaborative, and inquiry-based designs. If our quest is to succeed, we must eliminate our dependency on top-down mandates and our reliance on authoritarian dictates and rigid policies and procedures. Above all, we must eliminate the delusion that "one size fits all" can function as a controlling principle for education. We must work to overcome our failure to empower educators through teacher networking and collaborative, inquiry-based school cultures. To transform educational cultures and organizations, we must eliminate "paper and pencil" school improvement plans that do not organically guide and inform strategic planning; and we must eliminate incoherent, misaligned, and ineffectual testing and evaluation processes.

The capacity to sustain the loss of innocence—the willingness to admit that breakdowns require breakthroughs—is a critical part of the educator's heroic journey. We need to break down our inclination to cling to the comfort of the Shire, as the Hobbit, Bilbo Baggins, does when confronted with the call to adventure posed by the wizard Gandolf. Clinging to the familiar keeps us petrified and incapable of surviving in the face of change. As Deal and Peterson (1999) remind us:

Change always threatens a culture. People form strong attachments to heroes, legends, the rituals of daily life, the hoopla of extravaganzas and the ceremonies—all the symbols of the workplace. . . . Change strips down these relationships and leaves employees confused, insecure, and often angry. (p. 52)

To overcome the phenomena we have described here is to face the chaos and complexity of the change process head on. The willingness to take on that challenge is the heart of the next phase of the hero's journey: confronting the dragon at the door and the serpent in the garden.

REFLECTION CHECKPOINT: The Heroic School System

1. To what extent does our school system avoid quick fixes and panaceas to address complex institutional problems?

2. How have we communicated that one size does not fit all in the learning process? To what extent have we effectively supported our teaching staff to individualize instruction and accommodate students' individual strengths and learning styles?

3. How do we communicate within our system that mandates and policies are only as effective as the level of ownership and involvement we have encouraged on the part of all stakeholders?

4. How do we ensure that we do not rely only on experts and educational gurus to do our work for us? How do we institutionalize staff development programs and practices so that our school-based staffs can genuinely transform practices and instructional strategies to promote student achievement?

5. How do we plan for obsolescence? How do we avoid the tendency to add to our programs and curriculums without taking anything away? How do we make reexamining our priorities an ongoing process?

4

CHAOS AND COMPLEXITY THIS WAY COME

CONFRONTING THE DRAGON AT THE DOOR AND THE SERPENT IN THE GARDEN

> From ghoulies and ghosties
> and long-leggitty beasties,
> good Lord deliver us. . . .
>
> —ANCIENT IRISH PRAYER

> And what rough beast, its hour come round at last,
> Slouches towards Bethlehem to be born?
>
> —W. B. YEATS, "The Second Coming"

To walk the path of the hero's journey is to leave the state of unconscious innocence and move toward a conscious acceptance that we are living in times of chaos, discord, and disequilibrium. When we leave the stage of "innocence" (a word that literally means "without knowledge of good and evil"), we awaken to the reality of serpents infesting our Garden of Eden and fire-breathing dragons threatening to demolish the sanctity of our once-peaceable kingdom.

As we face the breakdown of idyllic innocence, we begin to accept that traditional approaches to solving problems and making decisions in education are no longer sufficient to protect us against the turbulent, evolutionary, and unpredictable nature of the change process. Confronting the growing expectations placed on contemporary schools, heroic educators entering this phase of the journey confront a bewildering list of social, economic, political, and psychological problems facing what was once "the little red schoolhouse" (Peel & McCary, 1997):

- An increasingly diverse population without a set of shared values and cultural experiences.
- Changing views of morality.
- An increase in self-destructive behavior in adolescents and young adults.
- Violence as an accepted fact of life.
- A technological revolution that is increasing the gap between the "haves" and "have-nots."
- The capacity for instant worldwide communication that is both empowering and overwhelming.
- New stresses on families, resulting in a decrease in the degree of emotional and psychological support that our children experience in their critical, formative years.
- The trend of looking to schools to provide the stability, emotional security, and basic care once provided by families.

Coupled with unprecedented social change, the complexity of forces that characterize the current educational reform agenda can lead educators to feelings of despair and alienation. Both of these psychological states seem inevitable at times in the face of the rising expectations and diminishing resources associated with schools as "last bastions" of normalcy.

In this phase of the heroic journey, we also begin to confront the "shadow" elements within our own organizations. As Stacey (1996) suggests, the shadow organization represents the unacknowledged and covert patterns of behavior that are in competition with the formal, overt components of a business or educational organization. In *Shaping Culture,* Deal and Peterson (1999) describe this phenomenon as the organizational subculture, consisting of informal leaders, "priests," "priestesses," "spies," "cabals," and the all-powerful organizational grapevine.

Schools in the midst of the chaos and complexity of their journeys need to confront the darker side of their organizations. They must squarely face the parts of themselves about which they are in denial. Facing our "shadow selves" as schools means looking closely at the extent to which our stated purposes and actions are at odds with our declared values. It also means acknowledging our limitations—our lack of knowledge and, possibly, our lack of will. Finally, it means surfacing the shadow organizations that may be operating within our legitimate structure: the gossip circles, cohorts of malcontents, the justifiably aggrieved, and others who wield covert power to negatively or positively influence the direction of a school. If we fail to recognize the shadow self within ourselves and our organizations, it continues to sustain a life of its own and stops us dead in our tracks on the path to substantive reform.

To grow in their journey toward integration and wholeness, organizations and schools must actively seek out the disconnects between the covert and the overt organization. People in the "shadow culture" can be called on to provide meaningful contributions to the school improvement process, if they are acknowledged by the formal leadership structure and brought into the dialogue. For organizational growth to occur, truth telling about the organization's reality needs to occur. All the parts of the organization that are not connected need to be reconnected for organizations to achieve their ultimate goals. Lacking reconciliation, members of the subculture, or shadow organization, will continue to contribute to organizational chaos to the degree that they are operating at cross purposes with the stated vision and mission of the formal organization.

In effect, no heroic journey can begin without the presence of phenomena that embody the "dark side." Chaos and complexity are the wake-up calls that challenge us to quest for new, creative, and more collaborative approaches to realizing our personal and shared visions for education. The problems, barriers, issues, and trends that populate the world of education today represent the dragons, serpents, shape-shifters, and tricksters found in myths and epics that make it *inevitable* for us to embark on the path of the hero's journey.

❖ ❖ ❖

Characters and forces embodying chaos, anarchy, and complexity abound in the great mythologies of the world. These personifications and representations of the internal struggles of humanity represent the darker, more sinister sides of ourselves and our world. If we fail to stand up to them and overcome their power over us, we lose our capacity for both personal growth and collective transformation.

Dorothy, the Scarecrow, the Cowardly Lion, and the Tin Man, for example, must summon the power of their individual and collective wills to defeat the enormous influence of the Wicked Witch. Both the witch and the Wizard of Oz himself are tangible projections of the protagonists' own fears, self-doubts, and lack of fortitude. In completing their journey, Dorothy and her compatriots discover their own magnificent power to transform their world. The Wicked Witch disappears—and the Wizard becomes mortal. In the end, they all can recognize both their individual and shared capacity for heroism.

Similarly, many of the worlds's great myths and legends are populated by monsters, demons, and chaos figures that embody the unresolved conflicts inherent in humanity. In the Indian religious classic *The Bhagavad Gita,* for example, the protagonist Arjuna—assisted by the disguised god Krishna—must confront his own self-doubts and fears in the face of the warfare raging around him. When he finds his spiritual center, he discovers his purpose in reestablishing order within the kingdom.

Other parallels abound, including the Hobbit Bilbo Baggins's discovery of his own ingenuity and strength in the face of defeating the trickster Golem and the fire-breathing dragon that ravages the countryside while protecting a supernatural treasure. Certainly one of the most memorable examples of chaos is Dante's confrontation of the punished sinners in *The Inferno.* Each circle of Hell is populated by human figures transformed into monstrosities, according to the nature of their sins on earth. Dante's poem reminds us to keep on the journey and to learn from the horrors we witness—overcoming our limitations and self-imposed restrictions in the process.

Overcoming our own limitations inevitably involves an extended period of struggle and testing. Luke Skywalker in *Star Wars,* for example, faces three forms of adversaries as he struggles to become a Jedi warrior. First, he combats the evil Empire itself in galactic warfare. At an even deeper level, however, Luke's darker side manifests in the self-doubts that plague him during his education under the tutelage of Obi Wan Kenobi and Yoda. Finally, Luke must grow to recognize, accept, and internalize the power of his greatest adversary, Darth Vader. Like the Wizard of Oz to Dorothy and her crew, Vader ultimately surfaces as just a man, rather than an insurmountable monster, as Luke demonstrates the power inherent within himself.

Perhaps no more powerful and fitting mythic metaphor for the struggles implicit in education is that of the Hydra, one of the monsters the Greek hero Hercules confronts in completing his famous Twelve Labors. This nine-headed swamp creature proved a particularly difficult adversary because one of its heads was immortal. When Hercules severed one of the nine heads, two more would grow up in its place. After heroic struggles with many heads, Hercules ultimately defeated the beast by burying the one immortal head securely under a great rock.

❖ ❖ ❖

Within the educational changes confronting educators and schools today, problems seem to beget problems, just as one hydra head compounds itself into multiples. Linear solutions appear inadequate in the face of geometrically expanding demands and issues. For example, introducing a new textbook series may seem to be a rational and logical choice for a school system, but chaos may ensue—and hydras formed—if the leadership does not provide sufficient resources for related curricular changes and professional development. Similarly, a board of education, facing tremendous public pressure and state demands, may mandate a new system of performance standards without considering the changes required in the infrastructure of schools (e.g., time, money, training, instructional modifications, and assessment changes). Once again, the hydra is unleashed, and chaos enters what appeared to be a rational universe.

The following are examples of how an urban principal we interviewed viewed chaos and complexity in education today. Here are the principal's comments on *external* chaos:

> On the external level, chaos and complexity manifests in such
> things as multiple initiatives, conflicting mandates, and the

diversity and transience of the student population. I hear my fellow principals saying: "Sixty percent of my 2nd grade students are going to leave by December. And then we will have a whole new group to assimilate . . . a whole new set of needs to be met."

This same principal described the *internal* side of chaos:

At this level, chaos and complexity take the form of self-questioning, conflicting emotions, internal confusion, and loss of focus. . . . For example, a new teacher comes in with a wonderful philosophy of what teaching is and the impact she wants to make. Then she is confronted with the reality of schools today with all their typical roadblocks. This causes internal turmoil and inevitable questions like: "Do I really want to do this? Is this really meant for me? Is this where I want to continue to put my energy?" When educators realize that it's not as simple as they thought—when they are thrown from innocence into chaos—they suddenly find that they are on a very steep learning curve. It's like in skiing. You think you are on the beginner's slope, and you suddenly realize you are on the double diamond with your skis pointing downhill over the edge of a cliff!

The Dragons of Chaos and Complexity as Signs of the Times

Why are the dragons of chaos and complexity such a pervasive part of our shared conversation in education today? Why do so many of us feel—either overtly or in our private, darker moments—that we are hanging on to order by our fingertips?

The good news, according to Garmston and Wellman (1995), is that these experiences are both inevitable and natural parts of the process of change and transformation: "The new sciences reveal to us that we live not in a world of *either/or* but *both/and*. Chaos and order are part of the same system; they exist simultaneously" (p. 6). Garmston and Wellman also imply that navigating this second phase of the heroic journey involves our willingness to embrace complexity in schools and in school systems:

We must seek patterns of order beneath the surface chaos and search for structures and patterns of interaction that release and amplify the energies within the system. To do so in schools, we must attend to twin goals: developing organizational capacities for adaptivity, and developing the professional capacities of all employees. (p. 10)

Hixson (1997) suggests that the chaos and complexity we are experiencing today in education results from living in a prime moment in history, a time when a whole new economic, political, and cultural world is emerging:

We are living in the midst of a paradigm shift where the way in which we identify our values, laws, and relationships is changing dramatically. Confusion and conflict proliferate during these periods, and there are no widely acknowledged rules of the game to provide stability, confidence, and understanding.

Hargreaves and Fullan (1998), in *What's Worth Fighting for Out There?* describe essential indicators of the chaos and complexity facing heroic educators. Suggesting that the pressures of today's complex environments are relentless and contradictory, they cite five major reasons for this increased chaos and complexity:

1. First, the instant access to information and heightened speed of decision-making that have been created by new technologies, significantly reduce our ability to foresee and control events.
2. A second cause of uncertainty and complexity in teachers' work also arises from the increased speed of information flow and decision making. Modern technology compresses time and space.
3. Third, even the knowledge bases that guide our educational responses to complexity are unstable. Knowledge about classroom learning, effective leadership or planned change, for example, is constantly being challenged.
4. Fourth, greater diversities of culture, language and religion in our student populations are throwing traditional educational goals into question and making consensus difficult to achieve.

5. Fifth, not only are outside pressures and demands on teachers increasing, they are also contradictory. . . . [For example,] the pressures of cultural diversity are leading policy-makers to embrace multiple intelligences and varied learning styles, while parents and some employers' groups agitating for "quality" education want greater standardization. (pp. 20–21)

(For an in-depth look at modern educators' struggles with such complexity, see Appendix B, "Perspectives from Real Life in Education.")

How, then, can the heroic educator, school, and system face the challenges of chaos and complexity? How can they successfully tame—or eliminate—their serpents in the garden and their dragons breathing fire at their doorsteps? In *The Living Company,* de Gues (1997) suggests:

To cope with a changing world, any entity must develop the capability of shifting and changing, of developing new skills and attitudes: in short the capability of learning . . . the essence of learning is the ability to manage change by changing yourself—as much for people when they grow up as for companies when they live through turmoil. (p. 20)

Chaos, Complexity, and the Heroic Educator

As in Hercules's struggle with the Hydra, the individual hero figure's confrontation with chaos and complexity typically takes the form of battles with a superhuman or nonhuman entity. One of the great appeals of horror movies is their ability to place us directly in line with one or more of these archetypal embodiments of evil. As we empathize with the heroic figure's wit, insight, and fortitude, we achieve—at least minimally—some form of catharsis, a temporary release of negative emotion as the heroine realizes her capacity for defeating the forces of anarchy and destruction. During the second phase of the heroic journey, however, the monsters, demons, and other personifications of chaos remain alive and well, testing the hero and forcing him to respond to the call and leave the security of the known, the protected but unconscious peace of the status quo.

The individual heroic educator can experience a variety of emotions and cognitive reactions during this phase of the hero's journey. "Chaos at the classroom level," Bennett (interview, 1998) points out, "is the individual teacher trying to make sense out of the hundreds of instructional strategies, tactics, and innovations that are out there." Bennett continues:

> One of the reasons for overload and burnout is that there is a tremendous amount being thrown at teachers all at once these days. People in policy positions don't understand what it takes to achieve substantive change. So they keep throwing down one thing after another. I don't know of any musician that simultaneously tries to learn to play every instrument in the orchestra. But that's what we're asking teachers to do. We're asking them to learn every instrument in the orchestra, and then we want them to go into the classroom and be the conductor. It's just not possible. It's almost like throwing a rock to a drowning person. Teachers are just beginning to feel skilled in a new practice and then Bang! a new idea, another curriculum, a new assessment, a new instructional model—just when they are coming up for air. (Bennett, May 1998 interview)

Several themes emerge as the heroic educator faces the chaos and complexity in the second phase of the heroic journey toward improvement in education:

1. ***Living Alone in the Dark Tower:*** Confronted with chaos and complexity, educators may experience a profound sense of personal and professional isolation. We may be left to our own devices to fend off dragons, serpents, and shape-shifters, with little if any help from colleagues and administrators. Teachers—especially beginning teachers—may feel that life in a school or school system is fragmented and lacking in clear goals, vision, and purpose.

2. ***Facing the Forces of Darkness Without Armor:*** Many teachers and administrators find themselves either unprepared or underprepared to face the challenges of change. Though the winds of chaos and complexity may be blowing, we may feel that we lack the technical knowledge, training, or support to meet the challenges we are confronting. The complexities facing us may leave us feeling vulnerable, unsupported, and powerless.

3. ***Clinging to the Known and Predictable:*** During times of stress and chaos, the individual heroic educator may retreat to simplistic or comfortable types of behavior and practice, rather than embrac-

ing the demands of the moment. When the system makes multiple and often paradoxical demands on teachers, some may remain fixated on the dogmatic, the rigid, and the controllable. From the perspective of findings in brain research, we may, under stress, limit ourselves to convergent, linear, and analytic thinking—and may miss out on the benefits of more creative, divergent thinking that seems threatening or beyond reach.

The phenomenon of teacher isolation is confirmed by many researchers. For example, Susan Rosenholtz's landmark study (1989) of 78 schools provided concrete examples of what is needed to increase student learning. She categorized the schools as "stuck," "in-between," and "moving." She used the term *learning enriched* (for both students and teachers) to characterize the *moving* schools. These schools exhibited four elements: shared purpose and direction, teacher collaboration, teacher on-the-job learning, and teacher efficacy. These factors were directly related to teacher commitment and increased student learning.

McLaughlin and Talbert's (1993) Stanford study, *Contexts That Matter for Teaching and Learning,* also found isolation to be a barrier to success. These researchers found that strong professional communities of teachers were able to successfully adapt to the needs of a diverse and demanding student population by holding high expectations for all students; by sharing knowledge of effective teaching practices in the content areas; and by engaging in ongoing assessment of their teaching practices. *In contrast*, teachers who worked in a context of *isolation* were *least* able to meet the learning needs of a demanding and diverse student population.

This experience of facing demons without suitable armor extends into educators' recurrent experiences with the Tower of Babel phenomenon, in which educators often lack a shared language or common vocabulary to describe what constitutes effective teaching and learning. The lack of consensus-driven language produces an isolation that is compounded even further by initiative overload and curriculum fragmentation. When the school system keeps layering on new programs and priorities, we can feel overwhelmed: "So much to do, so little time . . ." and "With all these conflicting signals, I'll just close my door and ignore them all."

Finally, the individual heroic educator must confront the "dragon" that disguises itself as nostalgia and longing for the simplicity of mythic "good old days." The tendency to revert back to what we know and are comfortable with keeps many of us from moving forward. We cannot solve present problems with rearview mirror thinking. One urban principal we interviewed emphasized:

> A dragon at the door is the fear that many people have of change. What makes it really complex is that not everyone views change in the same way. For some people in the system, or in my school, a particular initiative may be seen as an opportunity. For others, it may be seen as a threat—it becomes their dragon at the door.

REFLECTION CHECKPOINT: The Heroic Educator

1. To what extent do I currently feel that my professional life is inauthentic?

2. To what extent do I experience a lack of connection with the shared purpose, vision, and mission within my school and its system?

3. What would have to be different in my professional environment for my sense of professional isolation to be eliminated?

4. What technical knowledge do I feel I am lacking currently?

5. From what professional development would I benefit, to address the issues I identified in # 4?

6. In what ways do I operate at cross-purposes with other staff members because of our differences in our interpretations of the meanings of terms and the purposes of key initiatives within our school and school system?

7. What areas within my subject area, department, or grade level would benefit from our staff arriving at operational language to describe our shared understandings of practices that support effective teaching and learning?

8. In what areas of my professional life do I tend to cling to the known and predictable?

9. How do I deal with new or innovative programs and practices?

10. How might I modify any resistance or denial I might demonstrate when dealing with the change process?

Another principal we interviewed, Lorraine Monroe, described the experience some educators have when their attempts to make a difference deviate from organizational norms:

> The other dragon was fear. If I do this, what will happen to me? Will they take my job? Will I be declared as someone who is not quite on the team? I think you have to come into this work with a sense of yourself that is so strong that even when you meet caution and apprehension—the dragon that says, "Slow and steady, don't rock the boat"—you have the courage to say, "This is for the good of children, so I am going to do it anyway. Now if that means they will transfer me or say that I am incompetent, then I know I am working for the wrong system. The bottom line for me is doing what I know in my heart is good for children.". . . The battle scars can become beauty marks.

Chaos, Complexity, and the Heroic School

Beyond the level of the heroic individual, the heroic school and school system confront numerous examples of the chaos and complexity found on the great epic quests.

❖ ❖ ❖

Within the work of Homer, for example, chaos manifests itself as the phenomenon of war and its aftermath. Within the *Iliad*, the Trojan War becomes the backdrop against which all characters in that epic are tested. In the *Odyssey*, Odysseus, forced by ill winds into unknown seas, has to contend not only with the blunders of his crew, but with even stranger perils—the flesh-eating Cyclops, Circe with her deadly spells, the soul-chilling Land of the Dead—years of trials and temptations that seem always worse than the ones than came before.

❖ ❖ ❖

Bennett (interview, 1998) described chaos and complexity within the school arena in the following way:

> The serpent in the garden is our inability to take collective action using what we know about teaching and learning, classroom and school improvement. We know too much not to act. But we have a moral imperative: We are dealing with the most precious commodity in the world—our children.

Bennett also stressed that the chaotic phase of the heroic journey at the school level parallels many of the phenomena he associates with the sources of chaos at the system level:

> Chaos at the school and district levels are the multitude of variables that can affect quality implementation of a sound instructional innovation. . . . Chaos is trying to do too much too fast, so that nothing is done well or connected to anything else. Chaos is the lack of a sustained focus. It goes back to: What is your vision? What are your values? What are you willing to give up? What is nonnegotiable?

An urban principal we interviewed noted:

> I had the opportunity to move to central administration. It was there that I met the dragon. It was there that I realized how the layers of bureaucracy get in the way of innovation and change. What I met full force was the pervasive fear of making radical moves even though the radical move was truly the right thing to do for kids. The layer through which decisions had to pass was the political agenda of so many who were there. I think what disturbed me the most was how long it took for a great idea to get down to the people.

Finally, a state-level administrator described the incredible complexity of educational systems:

> The higher you move up in the system, the more complex it becomes. When I was a department chair, I thought the issues were complex. When I moved to the district level, they became more complex. When I moved to the state level, the complexity increased exponentially. There were enormous differences in resources. The differences in student populations we serve—from rural to urban to upper middle class. The differences in values across districts. The differences in dis-

tricts' readiness and capacity to change. . . . All of these contribute to the feeling of being overwhelmed.

Exactly what does this second phase of the journey look like at
the school level? Just as individual heroic educators at the school and
system level must confront the forces of chaos and complexity that
challenge and threaten them, school staffs must confront the dragons,
serpents, tricksters, and shape-changers that plague them, including
the following:

1. *That Old Devil Time:* The heroic school must inevitably confront one of its greatest adversaries—the lack of sufficient time to support the change process. In most schools, we find an agrarian and
industrial model of time in operation, with school calendars aligned
with cycles of planting and harvesting (hence, the vestige of schools
closed during summer months) and schedules aligned with assembly-
line practices (with a neat and consistent time slot for every subject
and activity). There is little if any evidence of time built into daily and
annual calendars for staff discussion, study groups, or professional development. Coverage remains the norm, while depth of inquiry becomes an inevitable casualty.

2. *Wandering Aimlessly in the Dark Forest:* Many school improvement plans remain paper products, at best; rarely are they organic, living documents that guide and inform the process of change
within a school site. In addition, many schools implement competing
initiatives and programs in a fragmented way in the hope of somehow
producing meaningful growth in student achievement. We wander
aimlessly in a dark forest whenever the purpose of change is unclear,
communication is minimal, support for quality implementation is lacking, priorities are unclear or competing, or collaborative planning is
replaced by top-down mandates and dictums.

3. *The Monster Without Teeth—Faulty Models of Professional Development:* The heroic journey can also involve problems
with professional development. Most of the current literature on
change within educational organizations emphasizes the critically important role of research-based professional development and ongoing
support for school-based staffs throughout the change process. Sadly,
school-based staff development practices rarely include what we

know works best in effecting, promoting, and sustaining purposeful change. Programs and practices often lack clearly defined purposes, sufficient time, long-term commitment, shared study and inquiry, action research, and a commitment to evaluating the relationship between training and changes in staff and student performance.

4. *The Unacknowledged Perils of the Shadow Organization:* Stacey (1996), in *Complexity and Creativity in Organizations*, points out that every organization, whether a corporation, school, or school system, has a shadow system operating within it. Those social and political interactions of individuals and groups that fall outside the parameters, values, and norms of the overt, traditional system comprise its shadow. According to Stacey, this is the arena in which members of an organization pursue their own gain, play out hidden agendas, and sometimes work to thwart official goals. And this is also the venue in which they may create innovations not officially sanctioned by the formal organization. The failure to acknowledge this shadow system, and to include its representatives in the change process being advanced by the primary system, results in breakdowns of the process and a lack of productivity.

All these indicators of chaos and complexity within the school site are present today: Schools experience insufficient resources, isolation, lack of shared knowledge, and inadequate coordination of initiatives. Most staffs would agree that perhaps the greatest challenge is to find the precious resource of time to ensure that purposeful change can take hold and sustain itself. Time becomes one of the great ogres, a not-too-subtle monster that deprives teachers of opportunities to share ideas, solve instructional problems, and collaborate. Because of how most schools traditionally allocate time, staff members frequently have little flexibility to plan together, observe one another teach, engage in study groups, dialogue about professional issues, and conduct action research.

Garmston and Wellman (1995) emphasize that effective school restructuring must involve redefining "the day and year to increase the time teachers have to interact collegially with one another" (p. 144). *Time as ogre* becomes even further compounded when schools do not structure time periods in the day or year to orient and train new staff members so that they understand the current professional development initiatives. As one urban principal we interviewed suggested:

> Even when you have a good staff development system in place, nothing ever stays the same. For example, we really worked hard on Dimensions of Learning, and for a brief period of time I had everyone moving along the continuum. And suddenly five people on my staff left, and five brand new teachers came in. For principals, the complexity becomes: "How do you bring them up to the same level as the rest of the faculty? And while you are bringing them up to speed, how do you also attend to other things such as new initiatives that come along? Or supporting staff as they are working on existing priorities?"

Chaotic Approaches to Professional Development: The Ultimate Dragon at the Door

The inability of educators and the public to translate professional development research principles into the reality of schools represents the ultimate "dragon at the door" of the untended garden of practices gone to seed. Continued failure to use the professional development knowledge base to guide practice threatens our demise. How is it possible to improve the quality of teaching and learning when we continue to set unrealistic time estimates for how much professional development is necessary to institutionalize change? As local, state, and federal educators and policymakers are developing mandates in the important areas of standards and assessment, for example, we find that people are paying very little attention to the time, skills, and resources needed to implement them. For whatever reason, decision makers continue to ignore those aspects of professional development that research and practice have shown to be the critical elements in promoting and sustaining substantive behavior change in instructional and administrative staff.

The one-shot training model is still alive and well in many places. Job-embedded staff development, on the other hand, is hard to find—despite the research that supports it. This kind of staff development is tailored to local needs and reinforced by site-based human and material resources. When policymakers, school boards, parents, and district leaders fail to recognize the importance of sustained professional development, school staff members face a sense of incredible fragmentation. In an interview, a state-level teacher of the year underscored this point. She referred to the phenomenon of "chaotic schools":

REFLECTION CHECKPOINT: The Heroic School

1. To what extent does time serve as a barrier to staff and student performance in our school?

2. What specific problems exist currently with our master schedule that work against student achievement and staff performance?

3. To what extent do we allow staff time in our school day, week, or year to encourage people to study new practices and programs and share their insights?

4. To what extent do we provide time for our students to do extended forms of inquiry and investigation, including laboratory, field, and library-media experiences to support them in completing independent projects successfully?

5. How does the way we use time in our building support—or work against—school-based professional development programs and initiatives?

6. To what extent is our school improvement plan a living, organic document that guides and informs our collective work to promote student achievement?

7. How does our school improvement planning process support—or work against—our stated long-range goals and annual objectives for staff and student performance?

8. How clear are we as a staff about the purpose, structure, and processes associated with significant change efforts?

9. How successful are we as a staff in communicating within and across subject areas, grade levels, and organizational structures about our shared purpose(s), direction(s), and achievement(s)?

10. To what extent do top-down mandates and dictums direct and control our staff's approach to problem solving and decision making?

11. How can we improve our approach to collaborative school improvement planning and instructional decision-making?

Chaotic schools are schools that try every program that comes down the road—the "do it and drop it" approach. When there is a new program, it becomes politically the hot topic. Thus we will look good to do this. We'll send a few people to a workshop. Everyone will get the stuff, told how we're responsible for doing it, and then it will never be heard of again. I know of schools where teachers say, "We never hear the same thing twice. That was then, this is now. We started the year saying this, and then we are told now we need to go to a new level, but we never hear anything about what was on the other level again."

So nothing is ever integrated with anything. And everything winds up being slapped on "top of" to the point that you feel utterly overwhelmed and fragmented. And none of it is focused on what will help the students learn.

For many educators, one of the greatest sources of chaos becomes outside pressures resulting from changes in direction, such as the ones the teacher of the year described. One principal concurred:

Chaos also happens when the system suddenly changes direction because of pressure from the outside. District leaders tell us to do one thing, they tell us to create a vision, they ask us to move along with a plan for staff development, but as soon as that vocal 1 percent of the community begins to make noise, they shift direction. Then at the school level we have to jump back and regroup.

This universal experience is much like the great mythic heroes and heroines who, like Dante at the beginning of his journey through the afterlife, find themselves suddenly having to navigate through fallen tree limbs and tangled underbrush in the "dark wood."

Chaos, Complexity, and the Heroic School System

The heroic system typically demonstrates several recurrent and interconnected patterns when it is undergoing the second phase of the heroic journey. In effect, the demons and monsters of this phase become the catalysts that precipitate the movement of the entire system toward greater resilience, effectiveness, and efficacy. They include:

1. ***Shape-Shifters at the Systemic Level:*** These quixotic phenomena include all the components that need to be aligned and mutually supportive of the system's vision and goals, but frequently are not.
They include systemic uses of time, resources, knowledge, staffing,
and coordination and alignment of efforts. School systems, particularly large ones, exhibit a lack of consensus about the purpose of education, conflicting operational standards for both staff and student
performance, competing agendas among significant stakeholders, and
the ever-present tendency toward the addiction of the quick fix and
easy solution.

2. ***The Trojan Horses of Systemic Reform:*** "What you see is
not what you get." In many schools, we see a disconnect between
what many educators and researchers *know* about promoting and sustaining change and what school systems actually *do*. A major pitfall for
many systems is often the propensity for innovation and novelty as a
solution to the complexities of the change process. Variations include
the love of symbol over substance—or the parallel tendency to cram
too much onto the change agenda. What do you get?—either a superficial and ineffectual approach to reform or a major addition to the system's cynicism and skepticism quotient.

3. ***The Shadow Knows, Part II:*** Just as schools have shadow
systems, school systems have them as well. A variety of covert but
well-sensed subsystems may work at cross-purposes with the overt, legitimate organizational structure that is publicly acknowledged by key
stakeholders and leaders. The shadow system can cripple or severely
limit the effectiveness of systemic change initiatives if it is neither acknowledged or if its creative, productive elements are not assimilated
into strategic planning and operations. The feeling we may have of a
balkanized educational arena is often the result of multiple shadow
systems operating at cross-purposes with the stated vision, mission,
and goals of the overt, legitimate part of an organizational structure.

Shape-shifters in the great mythic traditions tend to surface often,
particularly when a hero or heroine may be becoming too comfortable
or smug. These chimera typically take the form of any number of
manifestations of darkness and destruction; simultaneously, they personify the mutable, quixotic nature of the adversarial forces that the
world is quick to throw at the mythic heroes or heroines to test their

REFLECTION CHECKPOINT: The Heroic School System

1. At the system level, to what extent are we aligned in our collective understanding of our shared vision, long-range goals, and short-term objectives for staff performance and student achievement?

2. To what extent does our school system structure its use of time to support instructional goals and priorities? To what extent are we prisoners of time?

3. How does our district allocate resources? To what extent does the district equitably distribute resources to support clearly articulated systemic priorities and student achievement targets?

4. To what extent do we as a system appear to be working at cross-purposes or out of alignment concerning such issues as the purpose of education and educational agendas?

5. To what extent as a system do we avoid—or are we guilty of—a tendency toward the "quick fix" and the "easy solution"?

6. How does professional development support—or fail to support—our systemic goals, objectives, and instructional priorities?

7. To what extent do we use one-shot staff development sessions without appropriate follow-up and staff support to institutionalize change elements?

8. How do we use—or fail to use—best practices in staff development, including peer coaching, study groups, job-embedded practices, and action research?

9. To what extent has our district established support structures and processes to sustain the effect and institutionalization of professional activities?

10. How do we evaluate the ways in which staff internalize and use strategies and techniques presented in staff development programs?

11. To what extent do we as a system favor novelty and innovation without appropriate follow-up to sustain the change process?

12. Where within our system is there evidence of symbols over substance?

13. To what extent do we suffer as a system from initiative overload, cramming too many priorities onto our plate without the time and resources to sustain them successfully?

(Box continues on the following page.)

REFLECTION CHECKPOINT (continued)

---

14. What are the primary sources of skepticism and cynicism within our system? What solutions can we pose to address these areas?

15. What shadow systems appear to be operative within our overall school system?

16. How do these shadow systems work against stated systemic priorities, or how are they out of alignment with these priorities?

17. To what extent as a system are we balkanized, with multiple parts and initiatives working without a common set of purposes, performance targets, or operational processes?

18. How can we work to eliminate fragmentation and splintering within our district while sustaining meaningful and purposeful change?

---

character, strength, and commitment. In the case of the heroic system, shape-shifting often takes the form of mixed messages, signals, and allocations of time, resources, knowledge, and program coordination. It is compounded by a lack of understanding of the dynamics of the change process by high-level administrators, school board members, and state and national policymakers. This results in unreasonable legislative mandates for school reform, developed in a competitive political arena, where political gain is often achieved through "quick-fix" (but "no-win") solutions.

This tendency to place symbols over substance adds to the complexity of this phase of the journey. In a RAND Corporation-sponsored study of federal programs supporting educational change, for example, Berman and McLaughlin (1977) found that some school districts adopted external innovations for opportunistic reasons, rather than to solve a particular problem. Thus, the mere appearance of innovation was sometimes sufficient for achieving political success, rather than meaningful and sustained structural transformations. Uninformed attempts at reform can turn seemingly productive and useful initiatives into smoke and mirrors. This phenomenon contributes powerfully to school-based staffs' inclination toward cynicism and alienation.

What, then, can the heroic educator, school, or system do to move beyond this second phase of the hero's journey? The discrepancy between the perceived order in the ideal world of innocence and the chaotic reality of the world that emerges when innocence is "lost" often provokes the heroic educator, school, and system to ask: What exactly are we questing for? What will "getting there" look like? How can we bring order to the chaos around us? Inevitably, such questions lead to a call to become clear about priorities and a vision for the future. Those who choose to respond to the call begin their movement out of chaos into the adventure of the vision quest, the third phase of the hero's journey.

5

THE HEROIC QUEST

The Search for the Grail, the Jewel
in the Lotus, and Avalon

[This] stage of the mythological journey—which we have des-
ignated "the call to adventure"—signifies that destiny has sum-
moned the hero and transferred his spiritual center of gravity
from within the pale of society to a zone unknown.

—Joseph Campbell (1949, p. 58)

Any trip along your own path is a razor's edge.

—The Kana Upanishad

The heroic struggle to realize a vision greater than ourselves is as old
as the human species. The Neolithic hunter, searching for game to sustain his family unit, visualized the object of his quest through the great
bison and deer painted on cave walls by the shaman of his tribe.
Through this process of ritual magic, the vision of a successful hunt
sustained him as he confronted the perilous forces of nature. Similarly,
Native American, Australian Aboriginal, and African males marked
their rite of passage into adulthood and their emerging status of a responsible member of the tribal unit by venturing alone into the wilderness on their own personal vision quest. In the process, they
discovered the internal resources to sustain themselves in their con-

frontation with the transcendental powers that defined and shaped their universe.

The hero's struggle to discover the internal strength to sustain an external quest pervades all great traditions of mythology, folklore, and legend. This struggle is also at the heart of the journey of spiritual leaders throughout the world. It is common for great spiritual leaders to undergo multiple internal tests of faith and discipline as they seek to achieve their goals of compassionate service to others and mastery of their own inner lives. In reality, the hero's quest is the never-ending story of all of us, struggling to realize who we are and why we are here. The quest is a universal journey toward self-realization, mirrored in the lives of the archetypal figures of myth and legend. In facing and accepting the necessity of the vision quest, we align ourselves with heroes like Dante, Arjuna, Odysseus, Luke Skywalker, and Black Elk, who populate the path of a hero's journey that is as old as time.

Given the problems we face in education today, we need a heroic vision quest, both individual and collective, in classroom, schools, and systems. Our need for vision is fueled by the urgency we feel to find meaning and direction as we are faced with the breakdown of obsolete educational models and practices. This urgency has led us—both individually and collectively—to embark on the quest for answers and solutions to the problems confronting us. Like the quest of the mythic hero figure, our quest is personified by the search for our own Jewel in the Lotus, our own Magical Ring or Holy Grail.

❖ ❖ ❖

In both Hindu and Buddhist tradition, for example, the lotus is a spiritual flower allegorically symbolizing the awakening of the spirit: The veil of matter is pierced through spiritual discipline as part of the great metaphysical quest. The jewel discovered there as the lotus petals unfold symbolizes the higher self, revealed in all its glory through the spiritual hero's transformation. In education, our ultimate Jewel in the Lotus is the transformation of students and educators as schools and systems change toward humane, vibrant, and non-factory-like places of lifelong learning.

Similarly, the great symbol of the ring in world mythology is another apt metaphor for the heroic quest in education today. From the great Norse Ring of the Niebelung, which conferred untold power on its possessor, to the famous Ring of Invisibility in Tolkien's *The Hobbit,* the ring typically symbolizes some form of cyclical completion and wholeness. It is a reminder of the recursive and often deceptive nature of the mythic quest. Like the Holy Grail, the chalice that legend suggests was used by Christ at the Last Supper, the ring is a tangible object resonating with multiple layers of meaning and significance beyond its literal form.

Whether consciously or unconsciously recognized, the modern educator's quest involves a collective search for a way to make our schools and school systems heroic—capable of addressing the needs of increasingly diverse student populations and complexities associated with the social, economic, and moral demands that society places on our system of public education. Though our respective lotus, ring, or grail may vary in form, the underlying meaning of these symbols is becoming powerfully clear.

❖ ❖ ❖

What exactly, then, are we searching for in modern education? What are we committed to discovering about ourselves, both individually and collectively, and about how to make schools heroic as learning organizations? Our vision quest extends from our search for common standards and values. It also surfaces in our growing acceptance of the reality that untested theories, one-size-fits-all programs, and bureaucratic mandates cannot "save" us. We experience the pull of the vision quest whenever we struggle to make standards come alive in practice—whether content, performance, teaching, or professional development standards. The quest lives whenever educators re-examine the purpose of education in the face of public cynicism and pessimism about its current status as a social institution. We go on a vision quest whenever we commit to transforming the professional culture of our schools.

The vision quest is embodied in our search for ways to translate all that we now know about quality curriculum, instruction, and assessment into the daily lives of schools. It is evident whenever we struggle to ensure that all students receive an education grounded in the principles of excellence and equity. Of necessity, our quest involves the substitution of personal responsibility and an internal locus of control—a spiritual compass—for outworn, external rules and regulations. It involves giving up variations of the old themes of "We tried that before, and it didn't work"; "We are all in this alone"; and "You'd better do what I say." Our quest also necessitates aligning the "head" and the "heart" in education, an enduring commitment to ensuring that the total child (including her emotional, physical, social, and spiritual needs) is at the heart of the school renewal process.

Painting the Bison on Our Own Cave Walls

Just as the Neolithic hunter, preparing for the hunt, visualized the object of his quest through the bison and deer painted on the cave's walls, we also have our own "bison" or mental images in contemporary education.

What are the bison on our cave walls? As we embark on our vision quest for school transformation, what are the principles and mental images that guide and inform our personal, school-based, and systemic hero's journey? The heroic educators whom we interviewed—as well as an extensive body of educational reform and organizational renewal literature—confirm seven starting points for our journey (see Figure 5.1):

1. *Vision functions as a "field" within an organization.* Traditionally, planners and decision makers have viewed organizational vision as an end state, a linear destination. The New Science literature suggests that we view organizational vision quite differently—as an invisible energy field that needs to *permeate organizational space* (Wheatley, 1992). In this sense, vision becomes the guiding and informing field that brings order and purpose to the complexity that challenges organizations today. Some term this "energy field" the organization's *culture*—the values, beliefs, and norms that shape its vision. A principal we interviewed put it this way:

> It's amazing, but one of the things that the new teachers told us when they came to our school is that they could feel the way we lived and breathed our mission and goals. They said, "You talk it, you walk it, you do it. The staff know what's expected. And that permeates everywhere."

**Figure 5.1
Vision and the Hero's Journey**

1. **Vision functions as a "field" within an organization.** Vision needs to operate as an invisible energy field that permeates organizational space, influencing everyone who comes in contact with it.

2. **Vision building is an expression of hope.** Vision is an act of faith, in the midst of the doubt that surrounds us, that we can imagine and create a better future for our children.

3. **Vision is an expression of organizational and personal courage.** When we articulate a vision, we know who we are, what we stand for, and why we are here. We become fearlessly open with our values and beliefs.

4. **Vision building requires personal mastery and emotional intelligence.** The emotional intelligence that will sustain us on the journey involves self-knowledge, discipline, resiliency, and exceptional interpersonal skills.

5. **Vision building is an open-ended, dynamic process.** Our visions for the future are not set in stone. As we act and learn from our actions, our visions will evolve, mature, and grow.

6. **Visions need to be developed collaboratively.** Without the involvement of everyone in the school community, our visions become mandates without meaning. Our stakeholders feel discounted and marginalized. The result is a lack of understanding and commitment from those whose support we need most.

7. **The enactment of the vision requires personal responsibility.** Creating heroic schools requires personal responsibility on the part of every member of the school community—teachers, students, administrators, support staff, parents, the school board, and the community at large.

This is how Wheatley (1992) views the same phenomenon:

> If we can get vision to permeate throughout the entire organi-
> zation, we could take advantage of its formative properties. All
> employees in any part of the organization who bumped up
> against that field would be influenced by it. (p. 54)

2. ***Vision building is an expression of hope.*** The shared process of articulating and bringing into existence a collective vision for
education is both an intellectual and moral process. In effect, it is a re-
affirmation that despite the heartbreak and trials that we face daily in
schools and school systems, we can see that our actions can be purposeful and significant. It reaffirms the possibility of hope in the face
of despair, and light in the face of darkness. Vision is an act of faith, in
the midst of the doubt that surrounds us, that we can imagine and create a better future for our children. A national administrator we interviewed expressed it in this way:

> Much of our educational system is dysfunctional. Yet we are
> taking the stance of hope that it can be changed. To do this,
> there has to be a compelling vision, a burning platform, and a
> deep sense of discomfort.

3. ***Vision is an expression of organizational and personal
courage.*** The capacity for identifying and working collaboratively to
realize a shared vision requires moral purpose, strength of will, and
courage. It becomes a manifestation of our individual and collective
ability to bring authenticity and a brave new commitment to the workplace we share in schools. As Pearson (1989) notes:

> Becoming heroic means having attained a strong sense of self,
> an enlarged identity. We know who we are, what we stand for,
> and why we are here. We become fearlessly open with our val-
> ues and beliefs. Our life feels authentic to ourselves and to oth-
> ers. Gradually others become drawn to us, and our vision
> spreads. . . . As we begin to put ourselves out there and be
> seen . . . we attract to us people like ourselves who want to live
> in the same kind of transformed kingdom. (p. 152)

4. ***Heroic educators need personal mastery and emotional intelligence to be able to achieve their vision.*** Our vision quest cannot be sustained without a willingness to examine our own internal resources. Senge (1990) terms this examination the *discipline of personal mastery*. He calls it "a process of continually focusing and refocusing on what one truly wants, on one's visions" (p. 49). It is also a process of seeing things as they really are. Senge continues:

> It's a relentless willingness to root out the ways we limit or deceive ourselves from seeing what is, and to continually challenge our theories of why things are the way they are. It means continually broadening our awareness, just as the great athlete with extraordinary peripheral vision keeps trying to see more of the playing field. (p. 159)

The quest we embark on will be fraught with tests of our own ability to act with discipline, stay the course, deal with others, and combat our tendency toward self-doubt and discouragement. Thus our success will depend as much on our emotional intelligence (Goleman, 1995) as it will on our cognitive aptitude. The emotional strength that will sustain us on the journey involves self-awareness, motivation, empathy, resiliency, and exceptional interpersonal skills.

5. ***Vision building is an open-ended, dynamic process.*** Chaos theory suggests that the linear, stimulus-response thinking that characterized Industrial Age models of organizational reform is no longer sufficient to sustain our heroic journey. To be successful on our vision quest, we will need a new mindset about vision building. As Louis and Miles (1990) note:

> Visions are not a simple, unified view of what this school can be, but a complex braid of evolving themes of the change program. Visioning is a dynamic process, no more a one-time event that has a beginning and an end than is planning. Visions are developed and reinforced from action, although they may have a seed that is based simply on hope. (p. 237)

Fullan (1993a) advises that the initial process of vision building be regarded as open ended, so that a shared vision can eventually be shaped, reshaped, and refined as we grow to learn more about the change we are involved in. In addition, Fullan states that as our own knowledge and skill deepens, it is likely that bolder and more imaginative aspirations for the future will emerge. Thus, we must not view our image of the future as set in stone. Rather, we need a new mindset: As we act and learn from our actions, our vision will evolve, mature, and grow.

6. *Visions need to be developed collaboratively.* The process of vision development needs to be a collaborative one, involving all those who will be affected by the change. Perhaps the most significant thing we have learned is the importance of respectful involvement of all stakeholders in the vision quest, including students, parents, and community members. Without their involvement, our visions become mandates without meaning. Our stakeholders feel discounted and marginalized. The result is a lack of understanding and commitment from those whose support we need most.

7. *The enactment of the vision requires personal responsibility.* The essence of the heroic educator, the heroic school, and the heroic system is the courage to take unprecedented action on behalf of children. To be heroic, each of us must assume personal responsibility for translating vision to action. We cannot wait for others to do it for us, nor can we take shelter in scapegoating. Taking responsibility for enacting our vision and values, despite obstacles, is the essence of heroism on the part of individuals, schools, and systems. A teacher we interviewed stated:

> When you hit a barrier to your vision, you need to remind yourself that there is an imperative to the vision. You need to keep saying to yourself: "I'm going to do it anyway. I can't accept less." There is a fundamental moral imperative working here. This is about children. Once one person steps forward and does this, it makes it easier for everyone else.

(See Appendix B for other perspectives from real life.)

Setting the Course of the Vision Quest Within the Hero's Journey

The struggle to find purpose and sustain the vision quest in education resonates with the patterns and archetypes of the hero's journey. Lor-

raine Monroe, in her Keynote Address at the 1994 Annual Conference
of the National Staff Development Council, expressed the power of vision in this excerpt from the *Book of Common Prayer:*

> *Vision drives action.* You will realize the vision of your heart,
> be it base or beautiful, or a mixture of both. For you will al-
> ways gravitate toward that which you secretly most love. And
> into your hands will be placed the exact results of your own
> thoughts. And you will receive that which you earn, no more
> and no less. So whatever your present environment may be,
> you will fall, remain, or rise with your thoughts, with your vi-
> sion—your ideal. You will become as small as that controlling
> vision or as great as your dominant aspiration.

What, then, are the recurrent themes that emerge in the vision
quests of heroic educators today? The teachers, parents, and administrators we interviewed varied only slightly in the visions they described for themselves, their schools, and their systems. Their vision
statements were child centered and focused on learning. They emphasized the centrality of student growth, development, and learning as
the touchstones of their quests:

> I have only one vision. It's that our children will be able to
> have enough successful, healthy opportunities through all the
> pathways they encounter to be able to leave public school
> equipped for life.
>
> —DISTRICT ADMINISTRATOR

> My vision quest is for an educational pathway for every child.
> Where every child feels accepted and valued. Where every
> child experiences high expectations. Where every child has
> the opportunity to achieve his or her potential. The pathway
> needs to begin in kindergarten.
>
> —STATE-LEVEL ADMINISTRATOR

> My vision is to do something good for children, to make a dif-
> ference. To not let organizational politics get in the way of this
> ideal, which is to support children and to provide the best that
> I can for each child, regardless of what the formal regulations
> might say, regardless of what the current policy is. To stay true

to my values and maintain my integrity when my vision is
challenged.

—PRINCIPAL

The transformed school will be structured around the best that
we know about learning—not around how we get 2,000 kids
on school buses or how we field a football team. If the transformed school is structured around everything that supports
learning, the criteria that would drive every decision would be:
"How does this action support learning?"

—FORMER HIGH SCHOOL DEPARTMENT CHAIR

The Vision Quest and the Heroic Educator

The hero's journey in religion, mythology, literature, and contemporary film follows this same archetypal pattern: People have complex
and challenging circumstances imposed on them. In turn, they undergo experiences that test their moral fiber; commit them to a quest
bigger than any one person can handle alone; and, ultimately, with
the assistance of wisdom figures and helpmates, achieve a result more
powerful than any single path walked alone could produce.

What are the themes that can guide the contemporary heroic educator's vision quest? Both the extensive body of literature in the field
of contemporary organizational renewal and many of the interviews
we conducted reveal five recurrent patterns for this phase of the hero's
journey:

1. ***Personal Vision Building as a Sacred Commitment:*** In heroic journeys, the commitment to personal vision building—and the
enactment of that vision—assumes the quality and resonance of a sacred trust. As Block suggests in *The Empowered Manager* (1987), to articulate our vision of the future "is to come out of the closet with our
doubts about the organization and the way it operates. . . . It forces us
to take a stand for a preferred future" (p. 102). To be heroic, we must
continue to examine, reclarify, and reassess what is important to us
about students, schools, and the process of education. And once we
are clear, our commitment needs to be unwavering. We move from a
stance of neutrality to one of moral purpose. The real question is not:

"Is it possible to educate all children well?" Rather, it is, as Meier (1995) asks: "Do we want to do it badly enough?" (p. 4).

2. ***Shared Inquiry as a Cornerstone of the Successful Vision Quest:*** Just as personal vision building is a process, not an end point, we must hold both individual and shared inquiry as a value in our organizational and personal lives. As Fullan (1993a) suggests: "The conditions for the new paradigm of change cannot be established by formal leaders working by themselves. . . . Every teacher has the responsibility to help create an organization capable of individual and collective inquiry and continuous renewal, or it will not happen" (p. 39). In schools, the kind of inquiry that leads to bold visions involves internalizing the norm of continuous individual and group learning, whether that be by study groups, personal journals, portfolio development, or collaborative action research. Fullan (1993a, p. 15) notes:

> The formation and enactment of personal purpose and vision is not a static matter. It requires ongoing inquiry. It is a perennial quest.

3. ***Self-Mastery as the Ultimate Jewel in the Lotus:*** Collective realization of a shared vision for schools can occur only if members of the school community are dedicated to self-mastery. As Senge (1990) states:

> People with a high level of personal mastery share several basic characteristics. They have a special sense of purpose that lies behind their vision and goals. For such a person, a vision is a calling rather than simply a good idea. They see current reality as an ally, not an enemy. (p. 142)

This capacity ensures that the heroic educator can move on the path away from unconscious innocence and self-denial and confront the realities of chaos and complexity head-on.

Goleman (1995) suggests in his work on emotional intelligence that self-awareness, motivation, empathy, and interpersonal skills are essential for the resiliency that is a prerequisite for endurance and triumph within any life quest. In particular, notes Goleman, self-mastery involves the ability to be hopeful and optimistic despite setbacks. It means having goals, knowing the small steps needed to reach them, and having the courage and persistence to follow through. Self-mastery also involves self-knowledge. As Palmer (1998) says in *The Courage to Teach*:

> When I do not know myself, I cannot know who my students are. I will see them through a glass darkly in the shadows of my own unexamined life. And when I do not see them clearly, I cannot teach them well. (p. 2)

4. *The Capacity for Collaboration as a Prerequisite to Achieving the Vision:* A person on a heroic journey must have the ability and willingness to function as a member of a team. Fullan (1993a) states it this way:

> There is a ceiling effect on how much we can learn if we keep to ourselves. The ability to collaborate—on both a small and large scale—is becoming one of the core requisites of postmodern society. People need one another to learn and to accomplish things. (p. 17)

Similarly, a teacher of the year we interviewed said:

> If you have the vision, you know there is something more. You know you teach in a classroom that exists as a part of a school—as a part of a system that has to work together in a connected way. We don't teach in a classroom. We teach in a school.

5. *Vision and the "Razor's Edge of Paradox":* A recurrent theme among our interviewees was the recognition that to pursue the vision quest is to walk the "razor's edge" of paradox and contradiction. We risk butting heads and visions with individuals and groups mired in the status quo or the unconscious "innocence lost" of past programs and practices. For example, a teacher we interviewed said: "One of the biggest trials and tests is the isolation of the person with the vision by people who have made peace with the status quo." A principal said: "To retain your sense of hope and focus, you have to gravitate toward the people who still have the vision."

Many other people we interviewed echoed this concern about struggling to achieve a vision and collaborating with others, while facing the inevitable obstacles of resistance and nonvisionary practice. One department chair, for example, described her experiences this way:

> I once had a superintendent who told me that people on staff were concerned about my level of enthusiasm and hard work. "It's not natural," he said. "You must understand that many people are intimidated by you—you are like a bright light. And bright lights show up a lot of dust."

The isolation of the person with the vision was a theme that recurred in our interviews. One teacher stated:

> There are two characteristics that I have found to be common among heroic educators. One is an unquenchable passion. And the other is knife wounds in the back. If you have found a way to nurture yourself in creating your own unquenchable vision, then how do you find healing for the wounds? How do you deal with someone who says: "If I pull you down, I'll look better. Because if you're excited and passionate, what does that say about me?" It's a threat.
>
> If you are the one saying, "But the emperor has no clothes; there's a problem here," suddenly *you* can become the problem.

The educators we spoke with mentioned collaboration as an antidote to personal isolation during the vision quest—but collaboration with a caveat. They spoke of the need to monitor their attitudes when forming collegial relationships—the ability to be part of the team and, at the same time, to stand apart from the team when necessary. They noted that being collegial and a member of the team needs to be balanced with the commitment to be true to oneself—to articulate, even when in the minority, one's personal values and beliefs. A principal who has worked in international school settings told us:

> When faced with a moral dilemma, I often go back to my belief statements. They are written down in my DayTimer. Every time I've done that—gone back to my belief statements—people have been willing to rethink what they're asking, because they realize that I'm going to stand by what I believe. When you talk about your beliefs, you invoke power. People realize you are coming from a position of honor and integrity. This is how I deal with parents, with teachers, and with other administrators.

REFLECTION CHECKPOINT: The Heroic Educator

1. To what extent have I articulated my personal vision for myself and my role in education?

2. To what extent can I describe my vision for the purpose of education?

3. How would I express my values concerning the role that schools should play in the lives of their students?

4. What is my vision for a "preferred future" for my school and my school system?

5. To what extent do I demonstrate a capacity for personal and shared inquiry as a value in my professional life?

6. In what ways do I operate at cross-purposes with the expressed vision of my school and system?

7. To what extent do I contribute to shared inquiry and investigation within my school and system? To what extent have I overcome a tendency to be a "Lone Ranger"? How do I contribute to work groups and study groups within my work site?

8. To what extent do I reflect on and work to improve my capacity for emotional intelligence, self-awareness, motivation, empathy, and interpersonal skills?

9. How can I become more resilient personally and professionally?

The Vision Quest and the Heroic School

The heroic school, like the heroic educator, must embark on its own consensus-driven vision quest if true reform and transformation are to occur and be sustained there. In fact, the patterns and themes that recur in the educational reform literature and in the viewpoints expressed by our interviewees reveal striking parallels between the individual and organizational patterns required for a successful hero's journey:

1. *The Need for Shared Vision Building Within the Heroic School:* Just as individual heroic educators must commit to a course of personal vision building as a fundamental part of their professional practice, the heroic school must practice the process of shared vision

building. In *Improving the Urban High School: What Works and Why*, Louis and Miles (1990) suggest:

> [Visions] are not generated solely by the principal or another individual in a leadership position but, even where the principal is strong, are developed collectively through action and reflection, by all those who play active roles in the change effort. Visions become strong not because the faculty believe in the principal, but because they believe in themselves and their ability to really change the school for the better. (p. 237)

2. ***The Need to Implement Practices of Inquiry as Organizational Norms Within the Heroic School:*** In the heroic school, all involved believe that inquiry and shared investigation need to be the driving norms of learning organizations. Schools that overcome the barriers of tradition and time to engage in study groups and school-wide action research raise the bar and set the standard for others. These schools refuse to perpetuate norms of isolation. Instead, they embrace norms of inquiry, collegiality, experimentation, and continuous improvement. They believe that the construction of personal and organizational knowledge is a transformative social act. In this sense, they are truly heroic.

3. ***The Need to Promote a Capacity for Ongoing Organization Development Within the Heroic School:*** The heroic school has the capacity for self-reflection, ongoing analysis of its programs and practices relative to its vision for student achievement, and modifications of organizational norms and behaviors when needed. In heroic schools, personal growth and organizational growth go hand in hand. Teachers and administrators make a commitment to developing the facilitation skills needed to support organizational learning and change. They become skilled in group dynamics, team building, and meeting management. They are students of the research base on change. They are also skilled in data analysis and collaborative school improvement planning. They do not view their school improvement plans as exercises in paperwork to comply with district mandates. Rather, they see the plans they've developed as living documents that systematically guide action on behalf of the students they serve.

4. ***Collaboration: The Driving Force Behind Heroic Schools:***
Significant instructional improvement efforts are successful only to the
extent to which they are supported by the organizational culture of
the schools in which they are attempted. Research (Little, 1982; Newmann & Wehlage, 1995; Rosenholtz, 1989) has demonstrated that
schools characterized by collaborative work cultures; teacher on-the-
job learning; and norms of collegiality, experimentation, and continuous improvement have a significantly greater effect on student
achievement. Thus, heroic schools are characterized by a strong sense
of professional community among their faculties. In addition, these
schools open their doors to parents and the community at large. They
are collaborative internally and externally. The staffs of heroic schools,
working together to achieve a shared vision, have the courage to enact more authentic ways to provide everyone in the school community
a voice—including parents, teachers, students, support staff, business
people, school board members, and all other stakeholders. They are
not afraid to invite everyone to the table, including their critics—the
people and groups they most fear.

It is increasingly clear that the heroic path and vision quest undertaken by the heroic school cannot rest on any one person. The days of
the charismatic principal who can single-handedly transform a school
are gone, in part because education has a long and sad history of initiatives and reforms which died when the person who developed and
promoted them left. As Fullan (1992) describes in "Visions That Blind":

> The high-powered, charismatic principal who radically trans-
> forms a school in four or five years can be . . . misleading as a
> role model. This principal's strategy is fragile because so much
> depends on his or her personal strength and presence, which
> is relatively short-lived. . . . Too much store is placed in the
> leader as solution compared to the leader as enabler of solu-
> tions. (pp. 19–23)

In heroic schools, educators, administrators, and others view each
person as a learner and a leader. The principal's role, then, is to build
the capacity of others to learn and to lead. Louis and Miles (1990) note:

Hanging the fate of school reform on the communication skills of principals and superintendents alone seems to us a frail strategy. If the magnetic quality of personal leadership is absent, is a school condemned to being "dull, boring, and stupid"? We argue that it is not. (p. 218)

REFLECTION CHECKPOINT: The Heroic School

1. To what extent do the members of our school community share a common vision for the purpose and direction of education?

2. To what extent do we revisit our expressed vision and ensure that it guides and informs all facets of our decision-making and problem-solving processes?

3. How do we demonstrate that we understand that the vision-making and realization process is dynamic and ongoing?

4. To what extent do our collective and individual actions reflect our vision? To what extent are they at odds with it?

5. How do we communicate the values, norms, and organizational principles that define us as a learning organization?

6. To what extent are inquiry and shared investigation norms within our school? How do we involve parents and community members in these ongoing processes?

7. To what extent is our school improvement planning process a reflection of our understanding of the principles of organization development? How do we work to ensure that the values, norms, and practices of our school reinforce student achievement?

8. To what extent do our students perceive themselves as an intrinsic part of a learning community? When students demonstrate alienation and estrangement from the school and its organizational culture, how do we work to assimilate them?

9. How do we ensure that our organization development process is dynamic and organic, rather than static?

10. To what extent do we promote a collaborative work culture in our school?

11. How do we make use of peer coaching, study groups, and action research to eliminate staff and student isolation and to solve identified problems?

The Vision Quest and the Heroic System

Within the body of world mythology, systems typically manifest as kingdoms and empires. Vision quests, therefore, often involve a search for solutions to problems and predicaments facing vast regions and political and geographic boundaries. This search is like the vision quest in the heroic school system. At this level of the hero's journey, three themes emerged from the research literature and our interviews:

1. *Creating a Generative Paradigm:* As Kuhn (1962/1996) confirmed in his book *The Structure of Scientific Revolutions*—which introduced the term *paradigm* to the world—systems of thought, as well as organizational systems, tend to operate out of a collective set of beliefs and processes that shape their world view, judgments, and capacity for decision making. The heroic system must commit itself to creating a life-sustaining, organic, and open-ended paradigm, one that can encourage and not stifle the change process. Stephanie Pace Marshall (1998) suggests:

> I believe that the vision of education that we long for is the possibility to create whole, healthy learning communities . . . communities that liberate the genius and goodness of all children for the world, and that invite and inspire the power and creativity of the human spirit. It is our work to create a generative paradigm of learning that invites not only the fullness of our intellect, but the fullness of our imagination, the fullness of our emotions, and the fullness of our spirit.

2. *Engaging All Systemic Stakeholders in the Vision Quest:* Just as the heroic school must search for viable ways to turn the practices of inquiry into organizational norms, the heroic system cannot operate in isolation. In particular, it cannot ignore the various constituent groups and stakeholders that may be a part of the community it serves but who may express views contrary to those of system leaders. According to the New Science writers and researchers, the post-Newtonian world is a holistic, integrated universe; no parts stand separate from the whole. To operate as if they do is to operate in the world of illusion.

One administrator with a major national educational organization emphasized this principle:

> I think the biggest danger we face in creating a vision for education, in coming up with something that we have never done before, is doing it in *isolation* and then announcing it to the public. The heroic educator or the heroic system does not stand up alone. You don't stand up as the only ones who know we have a problem. Educators need to go public with their problems. We need to acknowledge that they are too complex to be solved alone. We need to stop fearing the public. They can become our greatest allies if we bring them to the table and make them a part of the process.

3. ***Viewing Change as a Guided Journey Without Blueprints:*** The change process is an open-ended and guided journey, not a linear process of neat cause–effect patterns with predictable outcomes. The heroic system acknowledges that strategic plans, neatly defined performance indicators, and job targets are our contemporary versions of "bison on the cave wall." They are useful forms of ritual magic; but, at best, they are approximations. We cannot prescribe the future. We must venture there together, using the lights, maps, and wisdom we can collectively muster, but realizing that no change process is linear, controllable, and orderly. In the post-Newtonian universe, where the link between cause and effect is tenuous, more-than-rational planning models are needed (Bailey, 1996).

At the heart of the heroic system is the vision of the school as a learning organization and the total system as a learning community. The underlying paradigm or world view that guides and informs that system's overall operations must reflect the best of what we now know about the change process. Transcending hidebound notions of learning as the acquisition of discrete, atomistic pieces of information, the heroic system's vision quest must involve the commitment to preparing all its students for a world dominated by transition, complexity, and challenge. As Marshall (1998) suggests:

> The learning community [we need to create] will be committed to increasing what David Perkins calls the "learnable intelligences." It will be comfortable with ambiguity and surprise. It

will be playful and trusting. It will be response-able. It will be love-able. But, most importantly for me, it will offer multiple ways of knowing about, accessing, and belonging to the world.

The capacity of school systems to promote, engender, and sustain the possibilities of learning for all rests in the collective aim of all stakeholders—including staff, parents, community, and above all, students—to envision the future as a realm of possibility and as a moving destination to which we are all traveling. In *The Fifth Discipline Fieldbook*, Senge, Roberts, Ross, Smith, and Kleiner (1994) describe a system's capacity for vision building: "At the heart of building a shared vision is the task of designing and evolving ongoing processes in which people at every level of the organization, in every role, can speak from the heart about what really matters to them and be heard" (p. 299).

How can the heroic system achieve its vision and use its change facilitators wisely? How can it both sustain itself and prosper throughout its vision quest? According to emerging brain research, the power of making sense of the future and of promoting the richness of its latent possibilities is virtually biological in its origins, manifesting in brain processes that compel us to assume this quest. In research published in 1985, neurobiologist David Ingvar of the University of Lund in Sweden confirmed that the human brain is constantly attempting to make sense of the future. As it does so, perceptions become embedded in memory. At the institutional and systemic levels, however, a company or educational organization is not wired to produce this sort of "memory of the future." Therefore, systemic leaders must take specific actions to produce one. All stakeholders must work collaboratively to improve a system's powers of perception—or they will not recognize events soon enough to avoid or minimize the effects of crises.

Ingvar's theory also suggests that organizations, corporations, and large systems can develop the sensitivity they need by finding ways to build up an organizational perception of the future. Increasingly, the heroic system will begin to make use of a variety of recently developed future planning tools. These tools acknowledge change as a guided journey without predetermined blueprints.

For example, de Geus (1997), in *The Living Company,* observes that Royal Dutch Shell, a company known for its remarkable longevity, has been using scenario stories and scenario planning since 1968 as part of their fluid, internally developed approach to strategic planning. Recently used by ASCD in its own strategic planning process, scenarios are tools for developing corporate *foresight,* stimulating discussions and documents whose purpose is not a prediction or a plan, but a change in the mindset of the people who use them. Scenarios develop and refine the powers of *seeing.* They help to perfect the art of perception among the members of an organization or system undergoing change and experiencing their own vision quest.

Interestingly enough, when de Geus (1997) describes his work with scenario planning in Fortune 500 companies, he says:

> I remind them to keep in mind that the best-remembered scenarios have some of the characteristics of fairy tales or folk tales. The mythological elements of the hero's journey, as Campbell noted in his book *The Hero with a Thousand Faces,* seem to resonate well for modern business people: The Departure, the Belly of the Whale, Initiation on the Road of Trials, and the Return . . . can all have parallels in scenario stories. In my experience, some of the scenarios that were best understood and longest remembered by the Shell organization had elements of Joseph Campbell's description of this timeless adventure. (p. 49)

The power of shared visioning and collective inquiry pervade the wisdom literature of all major world mythologies and religions. One of the great trickster figures in mythic literature is Anansi, the famous spider of West Africa's Ashanti tradition. One Anansi tale, "Why Wisdom Is Everywhere," gives us a powerful reminder of the need of the systemic vision quest to rely on the expansiveness of shared wisdom, rather than the restrictions and limitations of individual perspectives viewed in isolation (*Wisdom Tales from Around the World,* compiled by Heather Forest, 1996, p. 97). This tale reminds us of the wisdom of the young people for whom we create schools and school systems. It also serves as a reinforcement of the collaborative nature of the systemic vision quest—as well as a precursor to the next phase of the hero's journey, "Gurus and Companions Along the Way."

REFLECTION CHECKPOINT: The Heroic School System

---

1. To what extent do we all understand and have the ability to articulate the paradigm that shapes the thinking and operations of our school system?

2. How does our school system articulate and ensure a shared vision that we all support? To what extent do our system leaders share their vision for education?

3. To what extent do the norms, mores, and operating principles of our school system encourage rather than stifle the change process?

4. How does our system promote schools as learning communities?

5. To what extent does our system ensure that all schools successfully address the needs of all students, attending to their needs while promoting their individual strengths and personal visions for their future?

6. How does our system promote hope and possibility rather than despair and limitation?

7. To what extent does our school system engage all stakeholders in planning for the future of our students?

8. How does our school system promote norms of collaboration rather than isolation?

9. To what extent does our school system operate out of a recognition that change is a dynamic, open-ended process that cannot be mandated or prescribed?

10. To what extent does our system encourage creative problem solving and alternative approaches to decision making?

11. To what extent does our school system empower school-based staffs and the communities they serve?

12. How does our school system "manage the unknowable"?

❖ ❖ ❖

Anansi, the spider, had all the wisdom in the world stored in a huge pot. Nyame, the sky god, had given it to him. Anansi had been instructed to share it with everyone. Anansi looked in the pot every day. He learned how to make things of fiber, how to hunt and build houses, and how to live well with family and neighbors. The pot was full of wonderful ideas and skills.

Anansi greedily thought, "I will not share this treasure of knowledge with everyone. I will keep all the wisdom for myself!"

Anansi decided to hide the wisdom on top of a tall tree. Holding the pot full of knowledge, he started to climb the tallest tree in the jungle. He struggled to balance the pot in front of himself while climbing at the same time.

Anansi's son, Intikuma, watched with great fascination as his father struggled up the tree. Finally, he simply said, "If you tie the pot to your back, it will be easier to cling to the tree and climb."

Anansi heard this sensible advice but shouted in rage, "A young one with some common sense knows more than I, who has the pot of wisdom!" Anansi threw down the pot of wisdom in a fit of temper and disgust.

Pieces of wisdom flew in every direction. People found bits of wisdom scattered about and took them home for their family and neighbors. That is why, to this day, no one person has *all* the world's wisdom. People everywhere share small pieces of it whenever they exchange ideas (Forest, 1996).

6

GURUS AND ALLIANCES

COMPANIONS ALONG THE WAY

But when the People gathered once again around the fire telling the story of all that had happened, something new came to mind. "We have overcome the strength of Elephant," they said, "and our fear of Shark and Hawk. We have done this by sitting by the fire and telling stories of what has happened to us, and learning from them. Only we, among all the creatures, have the gift of story and the wisdom it brings. We do not need to be masters of the earth. We can share because it is wise to do so." From this day on the People held their heads high, never forgetting to sit by the fire and tell their stories. Never forgetting that in the stories could be found wisdom and in wisdom, strength.

—AFRICAN FOLK TALE

As this folk tale reminds us, there is great power in our ability to engage in collaborative dialogue using story, metaphor, and "wisdom tales" from our shared experience. In fact, an important part of the heroic journey involves the protagonists' ability to transcend their personal limitations by reaching out to companions of like heart and mind. The journey also involves a search for wisdom figures—individuals and groups who embody expert knowledge, insight, and truth. Ultimately, the "story" we create *in partnership with others* is the narrative tapestry at the heart of the hero's journey in education.

The archetypal tradition of transcendental helpers who serve as mentors and catalysts to bring out the greatness of the mythic hero and heroine pervades sacred writings through the ages. We see gurus, wisdom figures, and guides everywhere in myth and legend. This tradition is present, for example, in Native American and Australian Aboriginal vision quests in which the individual undergoing a rite of passage into adulthood navigates the wilderness assisted by spirit figures in the form of great and powerful animal figures. The bears, owls, coyotes, jaguars, cougars, and ravens of these vision quests retain their archetypal powers even today. When such figures serve as emblems and mascots for schools, they are totemic reminders of this tradition.

Perhaps the most famous guide and wisdom figure in the mythic tradition is Athena, the Greek goddess of wisdom, who assists Odysseus, his wife Penelope, and his son Telemachus throughout their struggles to reinstate order and stability in Ithaca. Disguised throughout much of *The Odyssey* as Mentor (a name, incidentally, which has become synonymous with the concept of a "guide on the side"), Athena provides support, encouragement, and insight into the proper course of action for each hero or heroine in Homer's epic. Like all great wisdom figures encountered on the heroic journey, however, Athena allows her proteges to make their own way and to discover the power that lies hidden within themselves.

Who are the "gurus" and wisdom figures that influence us in education—and why? How does external knowledge become successfully translated into internal knowledge? How can we tap into the collective wisdom that resides in ourselves and our schools, rather than only looking outward for the "savior," the panacea, or the scapegoat? Who are our traveling companions along the way, and how do they sustain us?

In this phase of the hero's journey in educational reform, we need to both seek out the wisdom of our colleagues and reach out to the insights of educational leaders and theorists for answers to the dilemmas we face. At the same time, the great myths and legends remind us that external gurus and wisdom figures are only projections and personifications of our own personal and collective selves. Our path leads us eventually toward internalizing any external, "transmitted" wisdom and insight. The novice or apprentice must become the initiate. What was once embodied in the physical form of the guru and her teachings becomes a part of the collective wisdom of the hero and his shire, kingdom, city-state, or—in our case—school.

The heroic path for educators today entails our joining together to study, internalize, and put into operation the best that we know about the teaching and learning process. Through shared inquiry, collaborative action research, and teaming, we can create schools that reflect key elements of cognitive learning theory and constructivism. In effect, the gurus and wisdom figures of this modern tradition—like Vygotsky, Gardner, and Senge—emphasize that knowledge is constructed through the individual's experience. As we add new knowledge and skills to existing cognitive schema, we expand our ability to perceive and judge our world accordingly.

Finally, our quest for knowledge must include ongoing dialogue with the people who travel with us at the heart of our heroic journey—*our students*. As Anthony Gregorc said when we interviewed him in 1998:

> Students are extraordinary teachers. They speak. They constantly tell us how our expectations, objectives, curriculums, and instructional strategies affect them. We need to look to our students to tell us why learning takes place—and why it doesn't. Our students are key sources for helping us identify what needs to be done. . . . Often we forget to ask them, and we forget to listen to the important messages they bring.

Gurus and Wisdom Figures: Who Needs Them? What Are They Good For?

The interviews we conducted for this book reinforced what we have learned from the current literature on organizational renewal and school reform. No single individual can transform what is essentially a collectively generated organizational system. The learner must, of necessity, internalize and come to "own" all externalized wisdom and teaching—whether that learner be a child or an adult. Specifically, the following major themes and principles emerged:

1. ***You cannot be heroic alone.*** It is impossible to succeed in the journey without kindred spirits and companions. When asked about gurus, the majority of interviewees mentioned friends first. They talked about their professional and personal network of friends. They rarely mentioned an "external" guru. They didn't talk about experts like Howard Gardner and Peter Senge. They talked about colleagues as the ultimate providers of mentoring and support.

2. ***Ultimately, external knowledge must be internalized and adapted to the needs of individuals and their school settings.*** As Wheatley (1992) emphasizes in *Leadership and the New Science:* "The physics of our universe is beginning to reveal the primacy of relationships. Is it any wonder, then, that we are beginning to reconfigure our ideas about organizations in relational terms?" (p. 12). The construction of personal and organizational knowledge, in fact, is a *social* act. Only through collaborative inquiry and dialogue with our companions along the way can we achieve meaningful organizational growth. We must combine *external research* with our own *internal knowledge* of the teaching craft, along with the knowledge of others in the school or system.

3. ***The polarities that we need to deal with at this stage of the journey have to do with collaborative team learning.*** Both benefits and risks are associated with having professional colleagues as our companions on the heroic journey. On the positive side, teams can learn from each other through analysis of problems and their solutions. On the negative, these same teams must face the danger of "sharing ignorance." How do teams decide when it is time to reach out to external knowledge bases, and when it is time to tap into the reservoir of professional knowledge that already exists within the individual, the school, and the system? And how can we get better at helping school teams find information, skills, and resources when they need them?

Another polarity has to do with the issue of "gurus" and purveyors of packaged programs. As we learn from mythology, it is important to be discriminating and to choose our gurus wisely. On the one hand, we know that there is a limit to what we can learn from external authority figures (i.e., no one "right" answer, no magic bullet). On the other, we know that we can learn from everyone, everything, everywhere.

4. *We know more about the need for collaborative work cultures in schools than we do about how to create them.* Why is it that the dominant cultural norm in schools is still isolation and privacy—despite all we know about the need for collaboration? Like a rubber band, we can stretch a school or system just so far—and then it tends to revert back to its original parameters, paradigms, and mental models. The true "heroism" of the journey is to break down the walls and dividing lines that prevent externalized wisdom from becoming internalized; that keep staffs from learning from one another; that keep teachers, parents, and community members from talking to each other; and that keep students passive and dependent. Creating collaborative work cultures is tough work, but it is the most important work heroic schools can do (Fullan, personal communication, 1997). (See also the extended interviews in Appendix B for more views on collaboration.)

The Heroic Educator: Gurus, Allies, and Companions Along the Way

The research, literature, and interview data we reviewed for this book revealed three guiding themes for the heroic educator in relationship to gurus, wisdom figures, and companions along the way:

1. *No external wisdom or knowledge source is sufficient alone to shape and inform our journey:* As the constructivist paradigm of learning takes the forefront in curriculum and instructional design, we need to remind ourselves that all knowledge is created by the learner. In effect, we teach ourselves; no one can "implant" either understanding or wisdom. Therefore, we must be aware that we can learn from everyone and everything we encounter. Bennett (interview, 1998) told us:

> Who are our fellow travelers and companions along the way? I guess they're the textbooks. They're the journals. They're the people we meet at conferences. They're our families and our colleagues next door. They are the kids and their parents. These are our companions. These are the people that sustain us.

2. *Teacher leadership can become the single greatest contributor to school renewal:* The literature of school reform constantly affirms the powerful role of the teacher as the heart of the reform process in schools today. External authority and wisdom figures, it turns out, have significantly less effect on the restructuring process than site-based teacher leaders. In *Awakening the Sleeping Giant: Leadership Development for Teachers,* Katzenmeyer and Moller (1996) note that increased teacher leadership is essential for school reform:

> We can no longer ignore the leadership capability of teachers—the largest group of school employees and those closest to the students. Empowered teachers bring an enormous resource for continually improving schools. School reform is dependent on teacher leadership being developed, nurtured, and reinforced both in the schools and throughout school districts. The potential for teachers to be leaders can be awakened by helping teachers believe they are leaders, by offering opportunities to develop their leadership skills, and by providing school cultures that honor their leadership. (p. 2)

3. *We must practice and model the process of being learners ourselves if we are to help students assume that role:* Educational reform rests in the capacity of staffs to be learners themselves and to share their individual and collective insights. Ultimately, we are in partnership with our students, learning from them, just as we expect them to learn from us. Heroic educators must be active learners, modeling for their students how they seek information, solve problems, and make decisions. Students must see in their teachers an enthusiasm and passion for learning. As Parker Palmer (1998) says, "We teach who we are."

A master teacher we interviewed said:

> When I first started teaching, I was hungry for professional knowledge. I needed all the gurus I could find. So I started experimenting with the ideas of experts like Madeline Hunter, Bruce Joyce, and David and Roger Johnson. All of a sudden I realized that there was a lot of collective knowledge out there. But it was also up to *me* to go out and collect it. There were few opportunities or support structures for professional

development in those days. People would say, "What do you do when your ship doesn't come in?" And my response was: "Swim out to meet it!"

There is no shortage of authentic and self-proclaimed wisdom figures in contemporary education. A difficulty is that the researchers and program developers often don't recognize the importance to the "consumers" of their wisdom of making connections across models, programs, and paradigms. So we tend to see their ideas and programs in isolation, rather than as vitally interconnected pieces of the complex puzzle of teaching.

Speaking of the urgent need for continuous professional learning, another teacher we interviewed said:

> I think that one of the keys to professional growth is to connect people to each other. You have to know where the other heroic professionals are so you can go to them to have your flame fanned when everyone else around you is trying to put it

---

REFLECTION CHECKPOINT: The Heroic Educator

1. To what extent do I personally avoid educational quick fixes and easy solutions?

2. How do I keep myself up-to-date on what the research and literature in my field are suggesting about best practices?

3. How do I make certain that I model and practice the process of continuous, lifelong learning as an operating principle in my professional life?

4. How do I make use of critical friends to support my professional growth and progress?

5. What is my relationship to my students? To what extent do we form a community of learning in my classes?

6. How do I model productive habits of mind for my students?

7. How do I structure my classrooms to ensure that we work collaboratively, rather than in isolation?

8. To what extent have I assumed the role of teacher leader in my school and school system?

out. And one of the hardest things is to have to constantly dredge up the energy to do that for yourself. Because you are unlikely to get systemic support for making those connections. We will know we've arrived "when that is happening."

And, finally, one of the principals we interviewed expressed the need to be tenacious in the quest for our own professional growth:

I believe you need to be your own mentor when all else fails. You need to develop an ability for incredible self-talk—an ability, at the lowest moments, to say to yourself: "I can do this."

The Heroic School: Gurus, Allies, and Companions Along the Way

One high school department chair told us: "The new paradigm for the 21st century is the heroic team. A team knows how to balance its strengths so you are all rowing in the right direction." Similarly, an elementary school principal emphasized the power of site-based empowerment, collaboration, and teaming, rather than dependence on external authority figures and top-down mandates:

I think when we go to the "gurus" to help us make changes we have to understand that whatever we learn will always have to be personalized within our own schools—that it can never be a recipe. Teachers need to take innovations and use them in a way that best fits their teaching style and their kids' learning styles. We can't all be walking around with other people's scripts.

The following themes emerged in the research reviews and interviews we conducted on the heroic school in relationship to gurus, allies, and companions along the way:

1. *Heroic transformation of schools requires a radical change in organizational culture:* True reform within the school inevitably involves the transformation of norms, mores, and standards in a school site. Significant instructional improvement efforts will only be successful to the extent that they are consistent with and supported

by the organizational context of the schools in which they are attempted. In the 1997 ASCD Yearbook, *Rethinking Educational Change with Heart and Mind,* Hargreaves notes:

> It was clear to us that the cultures of teaching should be a prime focus for educational change. A central task in creating cultures of educational change is how to develop more collaborative working relationships between principals and teachers, and among teachers themselves. (p. 1)

Alliances and companions along the way are particularly critical at this juncture. At the same time, external mandates and experts can give only limited guidance to this process. Wisdom and insight must ultimately emerge through the process of reflection, study, and collaborative inquiry with trusted colleagues.

2. *At the heart of true reform is the heroic school's commitment to a developmental focus:* Katzenmeyer and Moller (1996) suggest that if renewal is to occur, teachers must be engaged in the continual process of acquiring new knowledge and skills—and in sharing their knowledge with others. A developmental focus entails active mentoring of new teachers, time for teachers to observe and provide feedback through coaching opportunities, and job-embedded staff development. The latter process ensures that professional development is site-specific and sensitive to the needs of the adult learners participating in these experiences.

3. *The heroic school studies research-based practices that have been proven effective in promoting changes in school culture and student achievement:* This requires proactively reaching out to the educational knowledge base. It also requires that educators assume the role of being good critical friends, asking challenging questions and offering helpful critiques. Glickman, Allen, and Lunsford (1994) provide a summary of their research on several practices that work. Their study, conducted within the context of the League of Professional Schools, a growing network of schools committed to common principles, revealed that "high implementation" school sites were more successful than other participating schools because of three factors:

- shared governance that focused solely on teaching and learning (not on administrative duties and school management issues);
- a schoolwide (as opposed to teacher-by-teacher) approach to instructional improvement; and
- a process for collaborative schoolwide action research.

In *The Constructivist Leader*, Linda Lambert and her colleagues (1995, p. 102) support this finding by suggesting that educational leaders can influence school culture in positive ways by taking a dialogue-based approach to school renewal. This approach focuses on facilitating ongoing professional conversation that promotes relationship building and reflection, information sharing, a sustained direction, and partnering.

Sarason (1990) suggests that it is almost impossible to create and sustain over time the conditions needed for productive learning by students when these same conditions do not exist for teachers. Barth (1990) emphasizes that the strength of the relationships among the adults in a school has more to do with the school's quality and academic effectiveness than almost any other factor. What are the implications of these findings for schools seeking to become "heroic"?

Teachers in heroic schools would have greater discretion in making decisions on behalf of the children they know best. They would make these decisions with their colleagues in a climate characterized by respect and support. Joint teacher decisions would extend beyond the sharing of ideas and resources to critical reflection on the purpose and value of what they teach and how. Teachers would experience norms of collegiality and experimentation in their schools (Little, 1982). And finally, schools and districts would reconfigure time schedules so that a significant part of a teacher's workday could be devoted to job-embedded professional development experiences.

A principal we interviewed summarized her approach to integrating these principles and techniques into her attempts to create and sustain a heroic school through staff empowerment:

> My biggest priority is to keep a sense of perspective . . . and always reevaluate. If you've bitten off more than you can chew, jump back. If things aren't going along well, pull people in and talk about it as a staff. We continually explore where we need

to go and what we need to do. I've found that if you include the staff in all phases of your operation, if you include them in the process, they will do more than you ever thought they would. If you direct them to do this, do that . . . they're going to resist. Above all, we (as a staff) are committed to looking to see the connections among the initiatives we are trying. This approach reduces fragmentation. If our teachers can see that everything is connected . . . that it's all of a piece . . . we build an awareness that we, too, are involved as a staff in this complex process we call learning.

The Heroic System: Gurus, Alliances, and Companions Along the Way

The power of collaboration and the struggle to internalize wisdom appears within the heroic school as a miniature version of a broader system, what the medieval alchemist referred to as the *macrocosm*.

REFLECTION CHECKPOINT: The Heroic School

1. To what extent is team learning a fundamental part of our school culture and operations?

2. How do we use the process of collaborative action research to help us learn from one another and to solve performance and student achievement problems?

3. When dealing with change elements, how do we address the inevitable phases of the change process?

4. How do we ensure that we freely share information, rather than guarding it for a privileged few?

5. How do we demonstrate that our students are an active and ongoing part of our school's renewal process?

6. What role do educational reform leaders play in our thinking?

7. How do we avoid a tendency to use new ideas and programs as "magic bullets" to solve identified problems?

8. To what extent do we model and practice the principle that any new knowledge or skill must be modeled, shaped, and internalized?

9. How do we build in time for reflection and the work of critical friends as part of our school renewal process?

Throughout world mythology, the concept of "as above, so below" is evident. The great kingdoms and empires that are the backdrop for all heroic journeys are typically in as much transition and experience the same complexities as the individuals comprising them. This phenomenon is as true for school systems as it was for the Greece of Odysseus and the England of Arthur.

Without exception, the heroic journeys of myth and legend remind us that shared wisdom and commitment to collaborative, purposeful action are more powerful forces for transformation than any single individual's knowledge or skill in isolation. Mythic parallels to the struggles of school systems today abound. For example, Merlyn, perhaps the most famous of all wizards and wisdom figures in world mythology, is first a teacher to the once and future king, Arthur. At no time does Merlyn presume that he can intervene to prevent the incipient monarch from following his own path.

At a systemic/kingdom level, Merlyn may attempt to prevent calamity or chaos where he can, but he personifies the conviction that the guru and wisdom figure is a catalyst for the empire, not a force of control or direct intervention. In effect, the empire, the kingdom, the system—all must follow their own path. Ideally, this path will lead to insight and transformation. In his famous depiction of King Arthur's early years, T. H. White (1987/1996) in *The Once and Future King* describes the power of inquiry and the learning process:

> "The best thing for being sad," replied Merlyn, "is to learn something. That is the only thing that never fails. You may grow old and trembling in your anatomies, you may lie awake at night listening to the disorder of your veins, you may see the world around you devastated by evil lunatics. There is only one thing for it then—to learn. Learn why the world wags and what wags it. That is the only thing which the mind can never exhaust, never alienate, never be tortured by, never fear or distrust, and never dream of regretting. Learning is the thing for you." (White, cited in Palmer, 1998, p. 141)

Systemic Transformation

Good may ultimately triumph over evil in mythic tales, but only after the collective transformation of the individuals within the empire, kingdom, or system. Such a transformation derives from trust, honor, teamwork, a receptiveness to the inevitability of change, respectful communication, and shared leadership. These characteristics are intrinsic to both the mythic journey and the major patterns we found in the research and interviews conducted for this book:

1. ***Change at the system level, like school-level change, requires ongoing commitment to team learning:*** The heroic system facilitates the shared construction of knowledge. At its heart is a commitment to open and ongoing dialogue involving all key stakeholders, including teachers, principals, parents, support staff, and the community at large. When the system considers or undertakes new initiatives, system leaders include these stakeholders as part of the team. Parent education, teacher education, and student learning are cut from the same cloth.

2. ***Meaningful systemic change—at either the district or school level—requires that all teachers, administrators, parents, and community members understand the role of school culture and the dynamics of the process of change:*** Once again, the total systemic organization—whether at the community, district, or school level—must understand how successful change occurs. If every member of the system is a change agent, it follows that everyone must understand both the *content* and the *process* of change. They understand that it is a three-stage process—initiation, implementation, and institutionalization—occurring over time (years, not months). They also understand that changes in behavior and practice occur only when schools and districts provide systematic, planned support during the implementation stage of the change process. This is the critical juncture at which people can either slide back to older, more comfortable, but often less effective practices—or move forward to a new level of professional skill. Systems can shape their cultures to promote greater productivity and achievement, but only if all members of the system are at the table—and only if all members are working with a common language from the research base on educational change.

3. ***Organizations are living systems; therefore, the members of a school system must understand the critical role of information flow and feedback loops in shaping and defining their operations:*** We are living in the Information Age, yet many schools

and school systems still operate on an industrial model in which a few control information access for the many. A successful system within this paradigm is characterized by Micklethwait and Wooldridge (1996):

> A true learning organization is one in which knowledge ricochets around the system like a ball in a pinball machine. In other words, networks need to be built to shunt formal information from one end of the company to the other; moreover, barriers to tacit knowledge need to be discovered and removed.

Information is the lifeblood of a living system—whether a school, a district, or another kind of organization. Wheatley and Kellner-Rogers (1996) note:

> If information moves through a system freely, individuals learn and change and their discoveries can be integrated by the system. The system becomes both resilient and flexible. But if information is restricted, held tightly in certain regions, the system can neither learn nor respond. . . . When we shrink people's access to information, we shrink their capacity. (p. 82)

4. *Systems must ensure the presence of those conditions that support the effective operation of professional communities:* The research on effective change in education identifies certain key elements of successful schools, and school systems as learning communities. One of these elements is a professional staff with both technical competence and a commitment to working collaboratively for the success of all students. At the system level, this component also includes an articulated commitment to and demonstration of sustaining interdependent work structures. In their longitudinal research study "Successful School Restructuring," Newmann and Wehlage (1995) note: "When groups, rather than individuals, are seen as the main units for implementing curriculum, instruction, and assessment, they facilitate development of shared purposes for student learning and collective responsibility to achieve it." In professional communities in the Newmann and Wehlage study, teachers pursued a clear,

shared purpose for all students' learning. They engaged in collaborative activity to achieve their purpose. And they assumed collective responsibility for the outcome. This commitment, in turn, led to increased student achievement.

Cultural Norms in the Heroic System

The virtues and moral qualities embodied by the great wisdom figures become, in effect, the qualities that all of us must embody within the true heroic system. In their *Educational Leadership* article "Good Seeds Grow in Strong Cultures," Saphier and King (1985) declare that true systemic reform rests in the need to nurture the cultural norms that contribute to growth:

> School improvement emerges from the confluence of four elements: the strengthening of teachers' skills, the systematic renovation of curriculum, the improvement of the organization, and the involvement of parents and citizens in responsible school-community partnerships. Underlying all four strands, however, is a school culture that either energizes or undermines them. Essentially, the culture of the school is the foundation for school improvement. (p. 64)

The cultural norms that Saphier and King have found to be most closely related to successful school improvement initiatives have striking parallels in mythology. In the great mythic stories, heroes and heroines also join in partnership with others to achieve the object of a quest, to bring stability back to a kingdom, or to transform an empire. We see this phenomenon in works as diverse as the Arthurian legends and *Beowulf* and in such contemporary classics as *The Hobbit, The Wizard of Oz,* and *Star Wars*. The 12 cultural norms identified by Saphier and King as linked to school success, together with their mythological counterparts, follow:

1. ***Collegiality:*** Companions along the heroic path help one another and sustain one another in the quest, evidenced by the power of such archetypal colleagues as Luke Skywalker, Han Solo, Princess Leia, R2D2, and the Chewbacca, the "Wookie." Their individual strength is overshadowed by their collective will and commitment to bringing order and peace back to the Galaxy.

2. ***Experimentation:*** The heroic system encourages its staff to try out new solutions to problems and experiment with new ideas and techniques. The Wizard of Oz gives Dorothy, the Tin Man, Scarecrow, and the Cowardly Lion a seemingly impossible task, but through their courage and the synergy of their partnership, they discover the resources to not only endure—but to prosper.

3. ***High Expectations:*** Just as the heroic system holds staff accountable for high performance through purposeful evaluations, the great mythic heroes and heroines always find themselves accountable for voyages, tasks, and moral attributes beyond what they initially think themselves capable. From the hobbit Bilbo Baggins to the long-suffering Odysseus, Penelope, and Telemachus, this process results in not only their personal transformation, but the transformation of the world of which they are a part.

4. ***Trust and Confidence:*** Throughout the heroic system, leaders empower school-based staff members by encouraging independence and experimentation. The Arthurian cycle, for example, provides powerful parallels: Arthur's Knights of the Round Table are, in effect, his extensions, empowered to set off on their own vision quests as part of helping him to realize his spiritual vision for the kingdom over which he rules. Trust is the glue that cements the Round Table. When that trust is breached, all is lost.

5. ***Tangible Support:*** The heroic system supports and sustains growth by providing the time and resources for staff to develop and put into operation the knowledge and skills required to promote student achievement. Professional development that is ongoing, job embedded, and sensitive to practitioners contributes powerfully to this support process. From Krishna's ongoing support of Arjuna in *The Bhagavad Gita* to Virgil and Beatrice's support of Dante as he journeys through the afterlife in *The Divine Comedy*, benevolent forces ultimately support the great mythic heroes throughout their quest. Heroic schools can do no less.

6. ***Reaching Out to the Knowledge Base:*** Within the heroic system, knowledge bases are readily available for staff to access information concerning how students learn, research-based best practices, and discipline-based innovations. Skillful employees within the heroic system broaden their repertoires in relevant areas and appropriately align techniques and curriculum with students' needs. The great wis-

dom figures that populate the great myths—from Merlyn to Athena to Gandalf—all stand as ready sources of knowledge and insight to the heroic protagonists whom they encounter. Like Yoda in the Star Wars trilogy, the wisdom figures challenge their heroes to learn.

7. *Appreciation and Recognition:* Virtually every great mythic quest culminates in some form of final appreciation or recognition ceremony. At the conclusion of *Star Wars,* Luke and his team members are given formal recognition in a public ritual just as Arthur inevitably rewarded valorous knights in a formal court ceremony. In the heroic system, good teaching is honored within both the school and community. This recognition process can take the form of both informal and formal ceremonies and rituals.

8. *Caring, Celebration and Humor:* The heroic system encourages school-based staff members to show their caring for one another and awareness of significant events in each other's lives, as well as milestones in the life of the school. The great mythic tales of heroes and heroines are full of mutual caring, support, and humor. We see it in the loving concern expressed by the main characters in *The Wizard of Oz,* the quick-witted retorts and expressions of support evident among the characters in *Star Wars,* and the humor coupled with understanding—personified by animal characters that clearly reflect human foibles—in *The Wind in the Willows.*

9. *Involvement in Decision Making:* Shared decision making is implicit in the national movement toward school-based management and in the work of researchers who promote teacher empowerment (e.g., see Lieberman, Darling-Hammond, & Zuckerman, 1991). In effect, the heroic system empowers its staff by giving them a direct and ongoing role in key decision-making and problem-solving processes that directly affect them. The mark of true mythic heroes is their ability to make viable decisions about their own lives and the routes they will take on their uniquely individual quests. The emergence of Bilbo Baggins, Dorothy, and Telemachus as fully functioning decision makers reflects their growing status and ultimate spiritual and emotional transformation from innocence to heroism.

10. *Protection of What's Important:* In the heroic system, people continually try to protect the nonnegotiable requirements for effective teaching and learning to occur. Educational leaders protect teachers' ability to have sufficient instructional and planning time, pro-

fessional development resources, and access to suitable instructional materials—as zealously as Arthur guards Excalibur, Bilbo clings to his ring of invisibility, Dorothy protects her magic slippers, and Virgil ensures that Dante does not stray from the path toward Paradise.

11. ***Traditions:*** Traditions can narrow our focus and take us back (and sometimes *backward*) to the seeming security of the known if we allow them to run our thinking. The heroic system, however, regularly plans *new traditions*—events that staff and students can see as refreshing, challenging, or a definite change of pace; ultimately, these events can become a positive part of the productive traditions of a heroic school or system. Similarly, mythic heroes and heroines are initiated into the powerful traditions of the transcendental path on which they are now walking. Luke learns the traditions of the Jedi Knighthood, Dorothy internalizes the norms and traditions of the Land of Oz, and Telemachus learns the traditions associated with becoming both a leader and a mature adult in the absence of his father Odysseus.

12. ***Honest, Open Communication:*** The tradition of plain speaking is an intrinsic part of the heroic system, as well as the legacy of the mythic hero. It begins and ends with a systemic commitment to articulating and grappling with problems and decisions openly and honestly, with minimal obfuscation or deceit. Virtually every mythic hero and heroine personifies these virtues. Although they may begin in a condition of innocent unconsciousness—as Bilbo, Luke, Dorothy, and others do—the sincerity and pureness of their hearts allow them to be honest and ethical with others, ensuring the ultimate success of their respective heroic quests.

Principles of the Heroic System

Finally, the heroic system—like the mythic hero—is dedicated to three fundamental principles:

- the power of information;
- the importance of relationships; and
- the development of individual, group, and organizational identity (Wheatley & Kellner-Rogers, 1996).

REFLECTION CHECKPOINT: The Heroic School System

1. To what extent does our system avoid quick-fixes and "flavor of the month" approaches to reform?

2. Are consultants and educational gurus viewed as potential sources of information and knowledge rather than "having the answer that will save us"?

3. What role does information flow play in our system? How do we make certain that we take advantage of feedback loops within our system?

4. How does our system encourage teacher leadership?

5. To what extent does our system model the need to ensure that all stakeholders play an active part in problem solving and decision making?

6. To what extent do we ensure that information flow is productive and open ended? To what extent do we inappropriately restrict information access?

7. How do we capitalize on the innate drive and need to form relationships within an organization?

8. How do we reinforce positively and work to align the individual, organizational, and systemic identities that comprise our school system?

9. To what extent do we need to modify our approach to the 12 cultural norms that affect school improvement, identified by Saphier and King? These are the norms:

- Collegiality
- Experimentation
- High expectations
- Trust and confidence
- Tangible support
- Reaching out to viable knowledge bases
- Appreciation and recognition
- Caring, celebration, and humor
- Involvement in decision making
- Protection of what's important
- Traditions
- Honest, open communication

As Wheatley and Kellner-Rogers state:

> A system needs access to itself. It needs to understand who it is, where it is, what it believes, what it knows. These needs are nourished by information. Information is one of the primary conditions that spawns the organizations we see. If it moves through a system freely, individuals learn and change and their discoveries can be integrated by the system. The system becomes both resilient and flexible. But if information is restricted, held tightly in certain regions, the system can neither learn nor respond. (1996, p. 82)

The inclination of systems to shrink people's access to information results, according to Wheatley and Kellner-Rogers, in a shrinking of their capacity to produce and contribute to their system's productivity. Inevitably, this condition leads to the operation of "shadow organizations," as Stacey (1996) calls them. When people are starved for information, relationship, or identity, they always create or invent their own personal responses. The extent to which their responses are aligned with the system's vision, mission, and goals depends on the extent to which information flows, people in the system honor relationships, and all members' identities are positively aligned with system priorities. Wheatley and Kellner-Rogers (1996) note:

> In a world of emergence, new systems appear out of nowhere. But the forms they assume originate from dynamic processes set in motion by information, relationships, and identity. The structures that we work within, the behaviors we live out, the beliefs that we cherish can be traced back to what is occurring in these three domains. How we treat one another, how we work with information, how we develop our identity—these conditions generate all varieties of organization.
>
> Organizations spiral into form, cohering into visibility. Like stars on winter nights, they fill our field of vision and enthrall us. But organizations emerge from fiery cores, from richly swirling dynamics. This is where we need to gaze, into the origins that give rise to such diversity of form. (p. 87)

7

TRIALS, TESTS, AND INITIATIONS

STAYING THE COURSE

The sun turns black, earth sinks in the sea,
The hot stars down from heaven are whirled;
Fierce grows the steam and the life-feeding flame,
Till fire leaps high about heaven itself.

—THE VIKING EDDA

Do not seek to escape from the flood
by clinging to a tiger's tail.

—CHINESE PROVERB

The hero of myth, folklore, and legend undergoes a series of major tests and initiations that, at first, appear both external to that character and seemingly insurmountable. Ultimately, however, the hero realizes that the ultimate tests are often within. As Campbell and Moyers (1988) note in *The Power of Myth*,

> The trials are designed to see to it that the intending hero should really be a hero. Is he really a match for this task? Can he overcome the dangers? Does he have the courage, the knowledge, the capacity to enable him to serve? (p. 154)

Like the mythic hero, today's educators, schools, and systems face significant struggles and demands on their respective "Road of Trials," as

Campbell (1949) referred to this period of testing and initiation within the overall heroic journey.

❖ ❖ ❖

The trials and tests of this phase ultimately initiate the mythic hero into a higher level of personal development and a new sense of awareness of himself and the world around him. At the same time, temptations abound, luring the protagonist to deviate from the path and move backward toward innocence and denial—earlier, less demanding phases of the journey. In *The Hobbit*, Bilbo Baggins, continually longs to return to the security of his previous "nonadventure" life in the protected, pastoral womb of his shire. His tenacity and will to continue are tested perpetually by the fear and trepidation of his journey through the darkness of the world beyond it.

Similarly, Arjuna, the mortal protagonist of the sacred Hindu text *The Bhagavad Gita*, is tempted to forsake his sacred duty and turn from the chaos of the battle surrounding him. In *The Odyssey,* Odysseus undergoes countless tests of his tenacity, moral fiber, and will before overcoming them to make his final epic stand in Ithaca. Similarly, for Dorothy in *The Wizard of Oz*, her greatest test comes when she is isolated in the prison of the dark tower of the Wicked Witch, unsure of her own survival, much less her ability to return to Kansas. For each heroic figure, this period of testing and initiation is what St. John of the Cross labeled "The Dark Night of the Soul," an inevitable period of spiritual and emotional doubt and despair that may precede the breakthrough of insight, wisdom, and transfiguration.

❖ ❖ ❖

Like these mythic heroes, educators can suffer their own "dark nights of the soul," whether at the individual, organizational, or systemic level. It may involve despair over a perceived failure to meet the needs of one lost child—or of whole groups of students a school is struggling to reach with a higher level of service. At the school level, it may take the form of the heartbreak we feel at seeing children who have been physically or emotionally scarred since birth. At the district level, it may involve the need to deal with constant public criticism in times when community support, not blame, is desperately needed. As one educator we interviewed suggested:

> The trials and tests appear daily. As women, we know that. As a minority woman, I know that particularly well. There are the trials of being able to sustain the energy and sustain the will in the face of doubt or opposition. The buffeting from quarters where you least expect it . . . friends in high places who would agree with you when they were in front of you, and then undermine you when you were gone by not lending their full support to a decision that was really about children.

In other instances, educators may increasingly experience burnout and dark nights of the soul from *initiative overload* and *program proliferation,* resulting in cognitive disconnects, despair, and "giving up"—all internal tests of individual educators' strengths, will, energy, and sense of purpose. The current debate over curriculum standards and how to implement them represents a demanding test of educators' skill and will as we try to set content priorities in the disciplines while answering the ultimate question: What is most important for our children to know and be able to do?

Our journey in education involves challenging demands and, at times, overwhelming pressure to "stay the course" and sustain our vision. We confront rising expectations in a time of diminishing resources. And we struggle to overcome pessimism and cynicism as we face such phenomena as conflicting public expectations, an increasingly diverse student population, an alarming number of children in crisis entering schools unprepared cognitively or emotionally to learn, the inadequacy of the current structure to provide the conditions needed for all children to learn, and a growing sense that—in our attempts at reform—*we may have skipped a century.* As the 19th century paradigm of education dissolves, we recognize that we are searching for a 21st century alternative.

In the face of these overwhelming challenges, we are led to ask certain key questions: Will we be able to keep our feet on the path of the heroic journey in education? What obstacles might lead us astray? What are the inevitable barriers, problems, and change variables that we must confront on our path—at the individual, school, and system levels?

Some Touchstones for the Road of Trials

Some contemporary wisdom figures would advise educators to look at problems and tests with a new mindset. "Move toward the danger," say Hargreaves and Fullan (1998). "Problems are our friends," say Louis and Miles (1990). Gregorc (interview, 1998) notes:

> Tests are natural. Tests are constant. They are there to help us grow. They help us use our powers of discrimination to choose between good and evil. They are also opportunities for us to ask ourselves: Now that you've learned something, what are you going to do about it?

Gregorc also emphasized that we need to be clear about the terminology and words we use—such as *test* and *trial*. In our interview, he noted:

> The definition of test is: "An assaying or examining cup to determine the quality of a thing." On the hero's journey, we might say that in this cup are our experiences, and that we need to examine them to determine their quality. . . . Tests are opportunities to assess the quality of our behaviors and to examine our motives, purposes, purities, and strengths. They are the trials that prove whether or not we have learned the lessons the journey is teaching us.

In taking on the tests and initiations that are an inevitable part of the hero's journey, we suggest the following touchstones.

1. ***Problems are natural and inevitable.*** Problems are a part of life, a part of growth. There is no such thing as a problem-free change effort (Louis & Miles, 1990). As Bennett (interview, 1998) notes:

> When you talk about staying the course and maintaining our internal resolve, it's critical to understand that problems, conflict, and stress are neither good nor bad. They just are. Problems and stress are a part of change. They are a part of life. It's how we deal with them that turns them into a positive or negative force for making a difference in classrooms, schools, and districts.

Fullan (1993a) has found that successful schools do not necessarily have fewer problems. What they do have is better mechanisms for coping with them.

2. ***Problems can be our friends.*** Despite our instinctual tendency to do otherwise, many who have traveled the road before us suggest that we should view problems as opportunities for growth. As Fullan and Miles (1992) suggest, we cannot develop effective responses to complex situations unless we actively seek problems and confront the ones that are really difficult to solve:

> Problems are our friends because it is only through immersing ourselves in problems that we can come up with creative solutions. Problems are the route to deeper change and deeper satisfaction. In this sense, effective organizations "embrace problems" rather than avoid them. . . . Avoidance of real problems is the enemy of productive change because it is these problems that must be confronted for breakthroughs to occur. (p. 750)

Problems, then, are not just hassles to be dealt with and set aside. Hiding inside each problem is a workshop on the nature of organizations and a vehicle for personal growth.

3. ***School improvement problems can be grouped into three categories.*** Although at first they may seem as protean and inclined to shape-shifting as any ancient specter or chimera, problems tend to manifest themselves in three distinct forms (Saxl et al., 1990). They can result from (1) the *program*—its process, content, or population served; (2) the *people* involved, including their attitudes and lack of skills; and (3) the *setting*, including normal crises, competing external demands, powerlessness, inadequacies in the physical setting, insufficient resources, and, most important, ill-suited systemwide structures. Grouping problems into these categories allows us to select more appropriate interventions.

4. ***Learning occurs on the edge of chaos.*** From the perspective of the new sciences, contrary to our usual beliefs, chaos does not manifest itself in the natural world as total confusion. Instead, it is "bounded instability" (Stacey, *Managing the Unknowable*, 1992, p. 62). It is a combination of order and disorder in which patterns ultimately occur. Stacey notes that managers of excellent companies seek

bounded instability and use it in positive ways to provoke innovation (p. 79). Bounded instability is similar to what Piaget called "cognitive dissonance"—the experience of mental confusion when new information conflicts with our existing mental schema of how the world should be. It is precisely when people experience this type of disconnect—when their inner world feels "chaotic"—that they are most motivated to learn.

5. *"Wicked problems" will inevitably emerge.* Although problems certainly tend to share common characteristics and origins, the heroic journey inevitably involves one extreme type of problem—what one nationally recognized administrator we interviewed calls the "wicked problem":

> What you have to know about a wicked problem is (1) that you can't solve it alone and (2) if there is an easy answer to it, it's the wrong answer. To deal with wicked problems, you have to get the best minds, the people who know you the most, the people whom you trust and who will ask you the hard questions that make you think differently. Then you need to think about who you need to have at the table working on the problem, always remembering to ask: "Who else should we be talking to about this?"

6. *To solve problems, we need to lower the drawbridge.* When we are confronted by problems and crises, most of us tend to don our armor, gather our swords, and prepare our defense strategy. Productive change happens, however, when we move *not* into a defensive mode, but into a *relational* one. One administrator we interviewed suggested:

> There is energy that comes from more voices at the table. We need to recognize the power that comes from community conversations—from having dialogues about the truly puzzling problems in schools and classrooms, not about simple answers. People will come together in a school to talk about complex things, if we will let down our guard and allow them in. And this is also how we begin to build community again—the community that people long for. It isn't about pointing fingers. And it isn't about blame. It's about saying each of us is trying to do the very best that we can. . . . It

doesn't start by someone standing up and giving a PowerPoint presentation on test scores. It starts by saying: "This is what we know, and this is what we don't know. And these things are puzzles for us. We need all the help we can get."

(For more perspectives from educators we interviewed, see Appendix B.)

The Heroic Educator and Trials, Tests, and Initiations

On one level, the great mythic heroes begin in a condition of unrealized possibility. Their heroic journey may ostensibly be about saving a kingdom or an empire, finding some magical talisman, or seeking a sacred object like the Holy Grail. But that same journey presents a kind of alchemical cauldron in which—sometimes against their will—the heroes are thrown into unprecedented danger and adventure, pathways that will transform both them and the world in which they live. Luke Skywalker, for example, must leave the security of his farm to confront the tests that will allow him to be transformed into a Jedi Knight and restore freedom to the Galaxy. Bilbo Baggins must leave the comfort of his shire to become internally resourceful enough to survive his adventures and achieve a new self-confidence.

The good news—for both mythic heroes and heroic educators—is that the hero's journey always makes available certain magical spells, talismans, weapons, and amulets to ensure that we do not have to walk the path unprepared. In education, these "amulets" can be so obvious that we overlook them. A powerful amulet available to all educators on their journey is the literature on educational and organizational change, which offers guidelines like these:

1. *Heroic educators arm themselves with knowledge of the change process and with change-facilitation skills.* Saxl and colleagues (1990) cite six essential skills needed to facilitate educational change: The ability to establish trust and rapport with all members of the school community; the ability to understand schools and districts as organizational systems; the ability to manage the processes of collaboration, conflict resolution, problem solving, and decision making; the ability to identify and use internal and external resources; the ability to deal with problems as they arise with a wide range of coping

mechanisms; and, finally, the ability to develop the capacity, skills, and confidence of others in the school community to be change facilitators themselves.

2. *Heroic educators are thick-skinned and resilient.* Monroe (interview, 1998) noted:

> I will live doing what I think is right. If I am hurt by it, I have recovered before. Despite obstacles or information to the contrary, I choose to believe the best about people. You cannot do this work and have a divided mind, or the tension of always looking over your shoulder for all the negative things that might appear to block your path. I've been hurt many times, because I was so busy doing the work with teachers and children that I didn't see evil approaching. I had to come to terms with how I was going to deal with this. Would I change my behavior and be cautious or tentative? And I realized I could not live like that.

Commenting on leaders, Monroe said:

> I think people are pleased to have a leader who will not bend with every new wind or every new crisis. They need someone to count on—someone they know will stick to the central core of what is most important. And when that core is attacked, you stand strong. You stay the course, because you know you are on the right course.

3. *Heroic educators combat fear and discouragement by joining forces with others.* Like the individual and collective transformations recounted in all great mythic tales, educational renewal cannot be achieved by individuals or formal leaders working by themselves. In the great mythic journeys, it is only through the intercession, support, and transmission of key information by significant wisdom figures and allies (e.g., Athena, Virgil, Beatrice, Ben Kenobi, Yoda, Glinda the Good Witch) that heroes achieve their goals. Mythic heroes also survive because of the encouragement and help of friends (e.g., the Tin Man, the Scarecrow, the Cowardly Lion, Princess Leia, Han Solo). Heroes make sure that they do not become isolated. A teacher of the year we interviewed noted:

One of the major trials and tests is the isolation of the person with the vision . . . because that person is too threatening to those who don't think the same way. Individuals advocating change threaten those who have made their accommodation with the status quo. I think one of the most powerful things we can do is connect visionary people with each other. Without kindred spirits, without professional connection, we can wind up in burnout.

4. *Heroic educators create their own amulets and shields.* When we interviewed two members of the Comer School Development Program in Maryland, they talked about the "amulets, shields, and talismans" they used to deal with conflict and complexity:

REFLECTION CHECKPOINT: The Collaboration of Educators Within the Heroic School

1. To what extent does our school climate, culture, and organization reflect the belief that values are significant and should be expressed?

2. To what extent do our school improvement planning efforts take into account the complex, nonlinear nature of the change process?

3. To what extent do we avoid quick fixes and easy solutions to problems that are complex and multifaceted?

4. To what extent are shared decision making, problem solving, and inquiry a fundamental part of our school operations?

5. To what extent do we avoid the tendency to "tinker around the edges," with a consistent commitment to depth and clarity rather than quick fixes?

6. How have we helped parents and community members to become active and regular parts of our school improvement planning process?

7. How do we respond to those who resist a proposed change?

8. How familiar are we with the literature on resistance to change? How well do we understand the stages of concern that people experience when confronting the prospect of leaving comfortable, familiar practices to do something new? How will we go about getting more information on this topic?

The components of the Comer School Development Process that serve as our amulets and shields are the three guiding principles: Collaboration; No-Fault Decision Making; and Consensus. No-fault means that when a problem arises, you are going to approach it from a positive problem-solving position rather than spending hours trying to figure out who shot whom. . . . It shifts you to an entirely new place. Finding blame is not as important as accepting the responsibility to work together to fix it. When you are pointing your finger in blame, three other fingers are pointing back at you.

The Heroic School and Trials, Tests, and Initiations

Dealing with the chaos and complexity of organizational change—particularly the inevitable problems and conflicts—is a theme that pervades mythic literature. At the heart of heroes' capacity to deal with trials, tests, and initiations is their ability to align with a higher purpose that is shared by a larger group or society. Survival and triumph in the face of adversity require that mythic heroes be sensitive to the culture of the world they inhabit. Survival requires allegiances and alliances that provide emotional, moral, and spiritual shields against the capriciousness of the winds of change. Above all, success comes as mythic heroes are sensitive to individuals' strengths and needs when joining with them to overcome the dictates of fate. A teacher of the year whom we interviewed said:

One of the biggest problems we face is that education has been, by necessity, anchored in the past. Because schooling has always been about handing down the culture. Many educators see their role as passing on the wisdom of the past, rather than as opening the gates to the future. The challenge is [that] we can never fully know the future we are preparing our children for. So we have to use all of our collective wisdom to approach that task.

What Are Some Talismans for Schools?

The continuing nature of problems in education makes it particularly complex for school-based staffs to cope with problems. How, then, do we resolve problems and deal with conflicts when they arise?

What are the magical talismans, spells, and amulets that hold the heroic school in good stead when chaos and complexity surface? Research in the field as well as the interview data we collected suggest three themes:

1. *The heroic school works on establishing a culture of professional community.* The professional communities in which teachers work heavily mediate their responses to students and notions of good practice. In a Stanford University study, McLaughlin and Talbert (1993) found:

> Even the best teacher attitudes and responses have trouble enduring without a professional community to support, endorse, and validate them. Every teacher we encountered who was engaged in a high level of pedagogy belonged to such a community. (p. 17)

The study also found that teachers who were part of professional communities at the department, school, or district level were more likely than their isolated colleagues to change their practices. And *students benefit:* A longitudinal study by Newmann and Wehlage (1995) supported these findings by identifying the direct relationship between the presence of strong professional learning communities in the schools they studied and increased student achievement.

2. *At the school and system levels, heroic educators deal with trials, tests, and problems by putting into place new structures that support capacity building.* These structural components include the expansion of available time, resources, and ongoing training and support; removal of competing priorities; multiple forms of communication throughout the school and system; and networking with the wider environment and like-minded individuals, schools, and systems. Within the heroic school, the total school community understands that connection with the wider environment is critical for success (Hargreaves & Fullan, 1998). Successful schools are actively involved in seeking alliances, forming networks, responding to the issues of the day, learning from them, and contributing to them. Teachers in successful schools are more likely to value the sharing of expertise, and to seek help and advice both inside and outside the

school. They are committed to building their own skills. They accept that it is possible to improve. They are willing to be self-critical. And they have the shared belief, reinforced by the culture of their schools, that instructional practices can always be enhanced and improved. Thus they view professional development as a never-ending process, a way of life (McLaughlin & Talbert, 1993; Nais, Southworth, & Campbell, 1992; Rosenholtz, 1989).

3. *Heroic schools have a different mindset about resistance to change. They respond to it with respect.* Educators within the heroic school and heroic school system—from the classroom to state education agency—understand that resistance to change is a predictable part of the change process. It is a normal response to individuals' constructing personal meaning about the necessity or wisdom of changing behavior, practices, priorities, or beliefs. The organizational change literature provides research-based guidelines and practical options for dealing with resistance. The Concerns-Based Adoption Model developed by Hall and Loucks (1978) presents three predictable stages of concern people experience when confronted with change:

- *Personal* concerns ("What will this mean for me?")
- *Management* concerns ("Will I be able to do it?")
- *Impact* concerns ("What difference is it making in the classroom?")

Until the school or system responds with support for individuals' personal and management concerns, individual educators will rarely be motivated by concerns about the impact of the change on student learning. For a summary of the model and suggestions on how to support individuals at various stages of concern, see *Assisting Change in Education* (Saxl et al., 1990) and *Taking Charge of Change* (Hord, Rutherford, Huling-Austin, & Hall, 1987).

How Do We Motivate People to Change?

More recent work on change-adopter types of people is that of Everett Rogers (1991) in *Diffusion of Innovations*. Rogers suggests that people differ in their readiness to accept a change. Some will change quickly; others will take longer. He divides change-adopters into five categories:

1. ***Innovator:*** Eager to try new ideas, open to change, and willing to take risks. Usually perceived as naive or a little crazy and, therefore, not well integrated into the social structure of schools. Approximately 8 percent of educators fall in this category.

2. ***Leader:*** Open to change, but more thoughtful about getting involved. Trusted by other staff and sought for advice and opinions. Approximately 17 percent of educators fall in this category.

3. ***Early Majority:*** Cautious and deliberate about deciding to adopt an innovation. Tends to be a follower, rather than a leader. Approximately 29 percent of educators fall in this category.

4. ***Late Majority:*** Skeptical about adopting new ideas and "set in their ways." Can be won over by a combination of peer pressure and administrative expectations. Approximately 29 percent of educators fall in this category.

5. ***Resister:*** Suspicious and generally opposed to new ideas. Usually low in influence and often isolated from the mainstream. Approximately 17 percent of educators fall in this category.

What do heroic schools do with this information? Research and experience tell us that it is unproductive to label an attitude or action as resistance, because such labeling tends to place the blame and the responsibility for solutions on others (Fullan & Miles, 1992). For this reason, heroic systems approach resistance with a new mindset. They view change as a highly personal process in which people assess with their minds and hearts whether the proposed change is aligned with their own values and beliefs; whether the cost of changing is worth the proposed rewards; whether the change "fits" with the school's existing culture, vision, and practices; and whether the individuals perceive that sufficient support for building new skills will be forthcoming. Fullan and Miles note: "Any significant change involves a period of intense personal and organizational learning and problem solving. People need understanding and support for this work, not displays of impatience" (p. 748).

Thus, one of the most effective (and *heroic*) responses to resistance is to listen with respect. Listening honors the person who is having difficulty with the change. Empathetic listening to resisters' concerns sends them a message of consideration and respect. Attempts to argue with or discount what they are saying not only stops the information flow but also communicates that their opinions do not matter. The notion that *it is permissible to resist* may be a new experience for some people (Karp, 1988). Allowing people who resist change to express their feelings and concerns can go a long way in creating a positive climate in which they become more open to new ideas and practices. Conversely, trying to cajole or change resisters' minds through rational argument often tends to make the resistance more firmly entrenched.

Listening to a resister is truly a heroic act that requires patience, restraint, and excellent communication skills. The difficulty that change advocates run into when trying to respond empathetically to resistance is maintaining a balance between being understanding and flexible, while at the same time standing firm in their commitment to their own values and the new practices they believe are truly needed (Moffett, 1995b).

What Types of Problems Might We Encounter?

Heroic schools recognize that different problems require different solutions, and thus use many problem-solving mechanisms. Saxl and colleagues (1990) identify three closely-related problem patterns (evolving directly from the "concerns" noted previously) that appear in school improvement settings:

1. ***Program-Based Problems:*** These can include problems and conflicts associated with program processes, content, and target populations. They can include everything from unanticipated delays and a lack of coordination to planning failures, bad fit to the school, a lack of understanding among staff members, and a client base (either students or parents) who are unresponsive or hard to reach.

2. ***People-Based Problems:*** Typically, these problems extend from one of two sources—attitudes and lack of skill. They can manifest as resistance, skepticism, lack of hope, inadequate decision making and planning, and inadequate classroom methods.

3. ***Setting-Based Problems:*** These problems can range from normal crises to competing external demands, a pervasive sense of pow-

erlessness, and intrinsic limitations involving physical setting or available resources. Their origins can range from unanticipated events and confounding problems to district or state-mandated requirements; lack of control over hiring and budget; and inadequacies in facilities, space, time, and funding.

How Do We Cope, Anyway?

How can heroic systems develop the capacity to cope with such a range of problems? Saxl and colleagues (1990) identify the following options, in order of difficulty, for coping with the inevitable problems associated with change (pp. 5-25 and 5-26). They suggest that to cope with problems successfully, people and schools can use all these mechanisms. What is important is to ensure a good fit between the coping mechanism and the nature of the problem. The options are as follows:

- Do nothing.
- Delay action and move slowly.
- Continue doing things the usual way.
- Apply pressure (sanctions) and support (rewards, incentives, resources).
- Build personal capacity through training and development.
- Build system capacity through creating new structures (cadres of change facilitators; multiple coordinating groups; enhanced communication mechanisms; collaborative vision-building processes involving multiple stakeholders; flexible approaches to planning; balancing planning with action; and ongoing, sustained assistance).
- Restaff.
- Redesign the system (increase resource control; give more influence to roles and groups within the school; redesign roles; and redesign the organization, for example, extend teachers' calendar to 10 months to provide added time for professional development and on-the-job learning).

As noted previously, the problem-solving mechanism must be appropriate for the nature of the problem. Delaying or doing nothing should be used rarely, on an expedient or short-term basis. Doing things the usual way or applying increased pressure without support will not work for tougher problems. Creativity is essential (see Chapter 5, "The Heroic Quest"). Deeper impact comes from using problem-solving approaches that build personal and system capacity. The most heroic approach is to build personal and system capacity *and, at the same time, redesign the system.*

REFLECTION CHECKPOINT: Collaboration as a Norm Within the Heroic School

1. Within our school, to what extent are staff members at the center of the problem-solving and decision-making process?

2. In responding to systemic reform initiatives, to what extent do we ensure that all key stakeholders within our school are kept up-to-date and made an active part of the implementation process?

3. In what ways is our school a professional learning community?

4. When barriers or impediments arise that inhibit or weaken our ability to be a professional learning community, how do we deal with them?

5. How do we ensure that sufficient time, resources, training, and administrative support are available to reinforce staff-based inquiry, problem solving, and decision making?

6. How do we promote networking within our school and beyond it with other sites experiencing similar issues and problems?

7. How do we avoid a one-size-fits-all approach to problem solving in our school?

8. When problems surface, to what extent do we attempt to differentiate between their types and their causes?

9. How would we describe the coping styles evident within our staff when problems arise?

10. To what extent do we involve our clients—our students and parents—in our problem-solving and decision-making processes?

❖ ❖ ❖

The need for collaboration and mutual interdependence in the "Trials, Tests, and Initiations" phase of the hero's journey is beautifully summarized in an Ethiopian folk tale, "Fire, Water, Truth, and False-hood." According to this tale, Fire, Water, Truth, and Falsehood lived together in a large house. Although attempting to keep their distance, they inevitably experienced conflicts resulting from the distinctness of their individual characters and temperaments. When the four of them found themselves in the midst of a major confrontation, they brought the argument to Wind to decide who was master:

> Wind didn't know. Wind blew all over the world to ask people whether Truth or Falsehood was more powerful. Some people said, "A single word of Falsehood can completely destroy Truth." Others insisted, "Like a small candle in the dark, Truth can change every situation."
>
> Wind finally returned to the mountain and said, "I have seen that Falsehood is very powerful. But it can rule only where Truth has stopped struggling to be heard. . . . And it has been that way ever since."—(Retold by Heather Forest, *Wisdom Tales from Around the World*, 1996, pp. 91–92)

❖ ❖ ❖

The Heroic System and Trials, Tests, and Initiations

The cosmic systems that are depicted in the world of the great myths—from Dante's description of the afterlife in *The Divine Comedy* to Homer's presentation of the resolution of the chaos confronting the kingdom of Ithaca in *The Odyssey*—all depend on the alignment of their human and transcendental elements toward the realization of some greater purpose and vision. Trials, tests, and initiations within a school system parallel this process of transformation through their alignment toward a common vision and collective sense of purpose. At the same time, our predisposition to live in denial and resistance of-ten prevent the kinds of breakthroughs of which heroic systems are capable. As one teacher suggested to us:

> When a system has problems and is not working well, we know from the work of Deming and others that 80 percent of the time the problem is not with the people but with the sys-tem. The flaw is not in the workers so much as it is in the

structure of the system itself. So what should be done? Change the structure. We know enough to change the structure. We know a lot of people who know a lot about transforming organizations. We know schools that work. I just don't believe it's rocket science at this point.

How Can School Systems Pass Trials and Tests?

How, then, do we work together as a system to produce schools that work? How do we deal productively with the inevitable systemic problems that surface in all school systems, regardless of their size or complexity? The following major themes emerged in both our research review and the interviews we conducted related to the issue of trials, tests, and initiations within the heroic school system:

1. ***Effective problem solving and change management within the heroic system involve collaboration, vision, and transforming the organizational culture:*** Like the heroic school, the norms, mores, standards, and operating guidelines that direct the operations of heroic systems are at the heart of their capacity to identify, address, and revise solutions to problems that emerge within them. As in the hero's journey within the heroic school, becoming a heroic system means opening the doors of the system to increased collaboration. If dealing with trials and tests is ultimately a collaborative issue, what works against this process in most schools today? As one national educational leader suggested to us:

> A barrier is that we haven't made parents and the public our allies. We are too concerned with "looking good." We are not collaborative in solving problems. We are not collaborative in caring about the child. We need to extend our stakeholder group. We need to be more in tune with the external environment and the importance of relationships.

This same educator asked: "If we believe that schools reflect our community, we need to ask: 'Is our community at the table?'" In successful change efforts and problem-solving initiatives, the total school community works simultaneously on individual and institutional development. It fosters productive mentoring and peer relationships, team building, culture building, and cross-institutional partnerships (e.g., school community, school district, university, and business agency alliances), recognizing that the task is too big to go it alone (Fullan, 1993a).

2. *In an effective heroic system, information management is a critical part of dealing effectively with conflict, problems, and crisis:* Almost all the sources we consulted reinforce the power and singular impact of information access and management as a central controlling variable in the renewal and transformation of large systems. Whether an empire, a mythic kingdom, or a school system, increasing access to information by all members of a system sustains change and builds capacity. When groups or individuals in a system limit access to information or use it as a basis for power brokering and status designation, they foster a *bureaucratic culture,* to the detriment of openness, experimental inquiry, and the primacy of hope and possibility. The free flow of information in an organization is its lifeblood.

3. *Capacity building in the heroic school system involves thinking systemically:* Organizations are living systems that grow, learn, change, and adapt to their environments. A change in one part of the system (no matter how small) automatically affects all other parts of the system. For example, the simple act of one teacher's reaching out to a colleague to share ideas and information can have a ripple effect throughout a grade level, an entire school, and—most important—on the students in each of those teachers' classrooms. Thinking systemically means analyzing whether all parts of the system (e.g., curriculum, instruction, assessment, and school policy) are aligned to mutually support one another. It means that whenever we take action, we have a plan for assessing intended and unintended results. Finally, thinking systemically means that all members of the system are moving in the same direction, guided by a shared vision and a common operating language about what constitutes quality curriculum and instruction.

4. *Capacity building in the heroic school requires a paradigm shift in the system's approach to professional development:* School systems striving to be heroic place staff development at the top of their list of priorities. They demonstrate their understanding of the staff development research (Sparks & Hirsh, 1997) by translating that knowledge into action. This means the end of one-time, one-size-fits-all training events that are not part of a comprehensive and sys-

tematic staff development plan. Instead, when the school or district makes training decisions, planners have already designed ways to support educators in the quality implementation of desired knowledge and skills.

A new mindset also means that staff development plans are based on standards and place an emphasis on results. Trainers identify indicators of progress toward desired changes in teacher, administrator, and student behavior before they design the training. Finally, a new mindset about staff development means that policymakers will stop to consider the staff development implications of any new practice or legislation that is introduced (e.g., standards-based education and alternative approaches to assessment). While important, these are but the first steps on the journey toward becoming a heroic system. The ultimate act of heroism would be to extend teachers' contracts and alter the way time is used in the school day and the school year to allow for a rich array of internal and external professional development activities.

The mythic theme of transformation and metamorphosis is evident in the process of a school system's attempts to renew itself in the face of mounting problems and conflicts. Our interviewees emphasized that dealing with trials and tests at the systemic level requires that we transcend existing lenses and mental filters. An administrator in a prominent national educational organization told us:

> A fundamental barrier is that we cannot achieve the goals we are trying to achieve within the existing structure. We are talking about a totally new structure for education. A different conception of teachers, of time, of place, of professional development—and of what learning looks like, who's doing the learning, where "school" is. School is not a place, but we are still bound by the place.

The structure of the system and the subcomponents of its organization also play a significant part in the resilience of that system in the face of trials, tests, and initiations. In successful systemic change efforts, the school community understands that neither centralization nor decentralization works (Fullan, 1993a). The most successful cases of school change (Louis & Miles, 1990) have the following characteristics: two-way, top-down/bottom-up initiative taking, a low degree of district regulation, a high degree of school and district two-way communication, and strong district support and assistance in response to the school's own initiatives for improvement (Fullan, 1993a). Similarly, educators find that significant instructional improvements are possible only when the improvements are consistent with the culture of the *system* and when this culture supports the improvements.

What Are Amulets for a Heroic System?

In light of the multiple levels of systemic thinking required to effect change within the heroic system, five essential amulets and talismans are valuable for successful systemic reform:

1. ***Systems Thinking:*** This process requires that heroic change facilitators and teams identify gaps between the ideal and the real while using both single-loop and double-loop learning (Senge, 1990; Stacey, 1992). It is the process of *double-loop learning* that enables people to think outside the box, and that builds the capacity for innovation in systems.

2. ***Standards-Based Curriculum:*** Heroic change leaders within a system can use processes of back loading (i.e., identifying assessment standards and backward mapping to determine instructional interventions) and front loading (i.e., creating curriculum material first, assessments last). Out of these interconnecting processes, change facilitators create shifts in thinking and identify needed changes in their written and tested curriculums.

3. ***Research-Based Instructional Strategies:*** All staff should be fully informed and skilled, on a continuing basis, in using research-based best practices within the school and classroom, including innovations supported by cognitive learning theory, brain-based research, multiple intelligences, and cooperative learning.

4. ***Reculturing, not Restructuring:*** Transforming school systems requires that we transform how the system organizes and manages its subcomponents. Heroic systems, however, focus their major change efforts not on small changes in existing structures, but on major changes that will dramatically transform the culture of the organization, including its values, norms, beliefs, policies, modes of communication, and patterns of interaction. Reculturing means that professional development for everyone will become a top systemwide priority.

REFLECTION CHECKPOINT: Promoting Collaboration Within the Heroic School System

1. How do we promote collaboration as a norm within our school system?
2. What role does vision articulation play within our system? To what extent do all members within our system share a common vision for the future of education and our students?
3. How do we work to build a norm of trust and collaborative support within our system?
4. What structures and processes have we instituted to sustain a climate of mutual support within our system?
5. How do we encourage experimentation within our system? When a school, program, or person fails at something within our system, how do we respond? What are the consequences of failure for a person, program, or school?

---

5. *Redesigning Assessment:* Finally, heroic systems and the change facilitators working within them make use of many assessment techniques and repertoires to monitor and evaluate student progress and achievement. In addition to traditional tests and quizzes, the heroic system encourages effective use of performance assessment, student portfolios, projects, and demonstrations. Ultimately, educators in a heroic system emphasize the assessment of enduring understandings, practical applications of knowledge and skills, and lifelong habits of mind.

Pearson (1989) notes that overcoming the trials and tests of this phase of the heroic journey "fills us out and gives us substance. People who have taken their journeys feel bigger—even if they are small of stature. We feel the size of their souls" (p. 153). In her 1998 interview, Monroe told us:

> There is one wonderful thing about trials and tests. After you have passed a couple of them, you say: "Well, I'm just going to go on." The trials build a kind of self-confidence if you work

through them. This is what life is. . . . It's not going to be a smooth journey. Trials and tribulations make you strong so that you can take each one and say: "What did I learn from this that is going to make me change my behavior? What did I learn that tells me I'm not going to change?"

8

INSIGHT AND TRANSFORMATION

ARRIVING WHERE WE STARTED AND KNOWING THE PLACE FOR THE FIRST TIME

Is the work that I have described—
the liberation of the genius and
goodness of all children,
the creation of the new mind
for the new millennium,
and the creation of learning communities
that invite and challenge the wonder and
awe of the human spirit—
is *this* the work that you want to do?

—STEPHANIE PACE MARSHALL
(1998 ASCD Annual Conference General Session)

The ultimate purpose and outcome of the hero's journey is the return of the protagonist to her point of origin, knowing and contributing to the place in a new, more fully conscious way. The hero's experiences have been transforming and have equipped her with newfound powers of insight, wisdom, efficacy, and commitment. In turn, the individuals, empires, and kingdoms touched by the heroic figure as she continues on the path toward transformation are, in turn, transformed themselves.

As Campbell (1949) explains:

> The mythological hero or heroine sets forth from her hut or castle, is lured—or voluntarily proceeds—to the threshold of adventure. She journeys through a world of unfamiliar forces, some of which severely threaten her. When she arrives at the lowest point of the journey, she undergoes a supreme ordeal and gains her reward. The final work is that of the return. . . . The treasure that she brings restores the world. (pp. 245–246)

❖ ❖ ❖

After trials and tests that are both moral and physical, Odysseus, Penelope, and Telemachus are reunited at the conclusion of *The Odyssey*. The 10-year ordeal that they sustained results in a deeper sense of their own identity, and in a renewed sense of the enduring value of their relationship. Order is restored to Ithaca, and the rightful ruler is reinstated to the throne. In contemporary mythology, Bilbo Baggins returns home with a new-found courage, a broader view of the world, and in possession of Gollum's magic ring. Bilbo is no longer a "Hobbit who has never had an adventure." Similarly, in the final battle with Darth Vader, Luke defeats—at least temporarily—the Dark Side of the Force, both within himself and, externally, in the form of Vader, who is Luke's shadow self and alter ego. Peace returns to the Galaxy.

❖ ❖ ❖

In *The Hero with a Thousand Faces*, Campbell (1949) describes the end of the mythological hero's journey: "The effect of the successful adventure of the hero is the unlocking and release again of the flow of life into the body of the world" (p. 40). The final phase of the heroic journey in education can bring new life to schools. On the way, however, we must answer the following questions:

• What are the characteristics of a transformed educator, school, and system?
  • When do we "arrive" and what does "transformation" look like?
  • Is the journey a one-time event?

- To what "place" do we return?
- Based on what we learn on our journey, what is the legacy that we can offer to others as they embark on similar quests?

The hero's journey that we describe in this book is neither a one-time event nor a linear path. Like the paradoxes cited in quantum physics, the journey is a spiraling, recursive process. Pearson (1989) notes: "We keep circling through its archetypal manifestations at different levels of depth, breadth, and height" (p. 153). This view of the recursive nature of the journey of educational change was reinforced by a teacher we interviewed:

> We never really arrive at the point of being a hero, but we are constantly becoming heroic. We don't "get there." We are always "getting there." It's a cycle of growth.

Deborah Meier (1995), principal of the nationally recognized Central Park East Secondary School in Harlem, New York, reinforces the ongoing nature of the journey in *The Power of Their Ideas*:

> There's never a time when one can say, Well, I've done all that can be done. There is always something else. A child you haven't done quite right for; a family that is in unnecessary distress because of school issues; a teacher you haven't been a help to; a book, a game, an idea that might turn the tide. (p. 180)

Contradictions and Paradoxes

The world of the heroic educator, school, and system is riddled by questions, contradiction, and paradox. Recurrently, contemporary educators face three issues as they travel the path of the hero's journey:

1. *The Pogo Paradox:* As the cartoon character Pogo once remarked, "We have met the enemy, and they be us." The return within the contemporary hero's journey in education is the recognition that we are at the heart of the journey. True transformation within ourselves, our schools, and our systems rests with us. It will not occur if we somehow expect others to do it for us. The paradox rests in the re-

ality that both the positive and the negative—the good, the bad, and the ugly—are part of what it means to be human. When we accept personal responsibility for cultural and structural school change, we come to recognize the complexity and contradictions that are a natural and inevitable part of the change process.

2. ***The Peter Pan Conundrum:*** The transformation of schools and education as we know them will occur only when we "grow up"—when we overcome our tendency to remain attached to an earlier stage of development that placed responsibility for change outside ourselves. Clinging to antiquated mental models and paradigms about the way "things used to be" or "ought to have been" precludes our looking directly and honestly at the truth of our current problems and potential. By confronting the Peter Pan Conundrum, we grow up as individuals, organizations, and systems.

Maturity takes the form of personal efficacy and a capacity for collaboration, shared inquiry, and continuous improvement. With maturity we are able to see the big picture—how the classroom, school, and system are interrelated. Clinging to the factory model of schools that may have served us once but is no longer viable hinders us from successfully using the change principles and strategies available to us—many of which are presented in this book. We need to seek and create the knowledge to mature as individuals, schools, and systems.

3. ***The Wizard of Oz Insight:*** Ultimately, Dorothy discovers that she had the power to return to her home in Kansas all along. But it was necessary for her to have undertaken her adventures with her fellow travelers—the Tin Man, Scarecrow, and Cowardly Lion—to fully and completely internalize this insight. Like Dorothy, the heroic educator, school, and system open themselves to the experience of change to bring about ultimate renewal and transformation. We also come to realize our own inherent power and collective synergy, replacing a less-evolved tendency to rely on external authority figures and would-be wizards in favor of our own capacity for problem solving, creativity, and action.

To be heroic at the classroom, school, or system level is to accept responsibility and sustain the commitment for confronting and resolving the complex problems facing education today. Heroic educators and schools are like the heroes of Campbell's universal myth. They are men and women who have been able to overcome their personal, psychological, cultural, and organizational limitations to achieve a higher form of professionalism on behalf of students. As a former high school department chair and new state-level coordinator eloquently stated in an interview:

> A transformed educator, school, and system involves the ability of all of us to maintain persistence over a period of time—to not let the prevailing winds move us, but to stay true to our course. And within that persistence, it's also preserving our belief system and our integrity. We can't let changing circumstances—the crisis of the moment—dissuade us. The transformation at the end of the journey is a deepening of our belief system on behalf of children.

In mythology, the heroic figure often becomes king, queen, lord of the castle, princess of the realm. What does this mean for our time, a time that calls for collective heroism and responsibility? Pearson (1989) suggests that becoming royalty in our time means taking responsibility

> not only for our inner reality, but for the way our outer worlds mirror that reality. . . . This means that when our kingdoms begin to feel like wastelands, we know it is time to hit the road again and continue our quest. We may have become too comfortable. We may have stopped growing. (p. 153)

As noted earlier, we often enter the education profession in a state of innocence. We are blind to the complexity that is out there. Our visions are hazy and ill defined. We have no idea how, when, where, or by whom we will be tested. We don't yet know who our allies will be—or even that we will need them. The ultimate hero's journey is an internal one—from innocence to awareness, from psychological dependency to personal responsibility, from indifference to intentionality, from blindness to vision, from fear to courage, and from a stance of neutrality to one of moral purpose. As Joyce, Wolfe, and Calhoun (1993) note: "The fabric of schooling is cut from moral cloth" (p. 79). The real question, says Meier (1995), is not: "Is it possible to educate all children well?" but *"Do we want to do it badly enough?"* (p. 4).

At this stage of the journey, we must do what our heroes in myth do: "Seize the sword." Here, the hero takes possession of whatever he came seeking. Knights take up a sword, treasure hunters take gold, spies snatch the secret, a Hobbit finds a Magic Ring, an uncertain hero-ine seizes her self-respect, a Tin Man finds his heart, a slave seizes control of his own destiny. As Vogler (1998) notes, "The image of the sword is a symbol of the hero's will, forged in fire and quenched in blood, broken and remade, hardened, sharpened, and focused to a point like the light sabers of *Star Wars*" (pp. 206–207).

The sword, a symbol of the treasure the hero is seeking, often takes other forms. Sometimes the sword is a sacred object like the Grail, or an elixir that can heal a wounded land. Sometimes it is knowledge and experience that lead to greater understanding. Some-times it is the collective will to create something new, more beautiful and efficacious than ever existed before. (For perspectives from real life in education, see Appendix B.)

A Treasure Chest of Themes

Each of us who completes the journey will have a legacy to pass on to others. These are the lessons—forged in fire—that served us well. The following propositions (see Figure 8.1) regarding the transformed

---

Figure 8.1
What Is the Legacy? Propositions for the Heroic Educator, School, and System

The transformed educator, school, and system

- Approach change fearlessly.
- Know that their moral core is their shield.
- Have the courage to say no.
- Believe that "we teach who we are."
- Lower the drawbridge to their castle.
- Know that their strength comes from resiliency.
- View learning as their lifeblood.
- Believe that one act of courage can change the world.

educator, school, and system represent the treasure that is to be collectively ours at the last stage of the heroic journey in education.

1. ***The transformed educator, school, and system approach change fearlessly.*** We have conquered the dragon of change because we have had the courage to "move toward the danger" (Hargreaves & Fullan, 1998). We now understand the change process. Thus, it no longer threatens us. Like Dorothy, Bilbo, Luke, and Telemachus, we may begin in a state of unconscious innocence, but we grow to assume the mantle of determination, commitment, and vision, ensuring both our personal success and the ultimate triumph of our companions along the way. Like the ancient alchemists, we have turned our baser metals into gold, equipping ourselves with the moral courage to prevail in the face of chaos and complexity. In effect, we have mastered the knowledge base, acquired the skills, and used them to transform schools.

Even though we are more comfortable with change, we do not adopt every new idea that comes our way. Instead, we use our newfound ability to discern those changes that really matter, those that are aligned with our core values and beliefs, and those that have the highest probability of increasing student learning. Successful educational change, notes Fullan (1993a), is not the capacity to implement the latest policy. Instead, it is the ability to survive the dynamic complexity of planned and unplanned changes in an unstable environment while, at the same time, increasing the capacity of the school and its district to grow and develop as a cohesive learning organization.

2. ***The transformed educator, school, and system know that their moral core is their shield.*** A fundamental part of the hero's journey is a trip to some form of underworld that represents the darker, unconscious side of human experience. Dante experiences the horror show of the Inferno and Purgatorio. Luke and his companions undergo numerous tests imposed on them by the dark forces of the Evil Empire. Dorothy and her companions must also look deep within themselves to summon the courage to enter the dark wood, insinuate themselves into the witch's castle, and return to the Wizard of Oz with the treasured broomstick.

Like all great mythic heroes who confront the darker, unacknowledged sides of themselves, heroic educators have achieved alignment between who they say they are, who they wish to become, and who they tend to be in practice. They have a sense of themselves so strong that, even when they meet caution and apprehension—even when they meet the dragon that says, "Slow and steady. . . . Don't rock the boat," they have the courage to say, "This is for the good of children, so I am going to do it anyway" (Monroe, interview, 1998). Having survived tests that challenged their moral fiber, these educators now stand strong.

    3. *The transformed educator, school, and system have the courage to say no.* Teaching at its core is a moral enterprise. Its purpose is to make a difference in the lives of students—*all* students, regardless of class, gender, socioeconomic status, or ethnicity. When educators leave the "state of innocence" (a state that is literally "without knowledge of good and evil"), they become conscious of the world as it is. With this new consciousness, they are called to make choices. They become responsible for their actions. To deny that responsibility is to become "unconscious" again, to revert to a lower level of one's being (Gregorc, interview, 1998).

    What does it mean to be heroic when we are faced with decisions, policies, behaviors, priorities, structures, and practices that are not fundamentally good for all children? In response to this question, a teacher we interviewed said:

> At some point, heroic educators need to stand up and say, "No!" If this violates our values and goes against our calling of who we are and what we stand for as educators, we need to stand up and be counted. To constantly acquiesce to a dysfunctional system, or to structural inadequacy, is wrong. Heroism is about personal responsibility. It's about people who choose to assume an internal locus of control—instead of those who say: "If only . . . " or "Yes, but. . . ."

The courage to say no is an expression of moral purpose. Other people—even within our own school or system—frequently test our purpose. As an international education consultant suggested:

> A test of moral purpose is when we have the opportunity to speak out against something we know is wrong, and we choose not to. It's when we remain silent. Or when we leave.

In the teacher's lounge, it is not speaking out when we hear others blaming a child or criticizing a teacher. Doing nothing is failing the test.

4. ***Transformed educators, schools, and systems lower the drawbridge to the castle and know that their strength comes from relationships.*** Lowering the drawbridge to the district requires allowing others to enter the school and the classroom. It means lowering our defenses, being open to communication, feedback, and new sources of knowledge. Because heroic educators know that they can learn from everyone and everything, they open the doors to their schools and invite the community in. They physically open the doors to their classrooms and invite their colleagues in. They act as mentors and coaches. They observe each other teach. They form study groups. They visit other classrooms in other schools. They begin to become instructional leaders—formally and informally. Heroic principals do the same. Heroic teachers and principals lead within and beyond the classroom and school. They influence others toward improved educational practice. And they contribute to a community of leaders (Katzenmeyer & Moller, 1996).

Wheatley (1992) suggests that "power in organizations is the capacity generated by relationships" (p. 39). Like all dynamic, organic, living systems, organizations need strong relationships to evolve and grow. As Wheatley notes:

> All of us will need better skills in listening, communicating, and facilitating groups, because these are talents that build strong relationships. It is well known that the era of the rugged individualist has been replaced by the era of the team player. . . . The quantum world has demolished the concept of the unconnected individual. (p. 38)

5. ***Transformed educators, schools, and systems know that their power comes from resiliency.*** To survive the hero's journey, to become heroes and not martyrs, educators, schools, and systems need to become "emotionally intelligent" (Goleman, 1995). Hargreaves and Fullan (1998) describe three kinds of support that contribute to personal and collective resilience in the face of change: "good relationships; connections in the community; and a transcendent value

system" (p. 117). They suggest being aware of one's own feelings and the feelings of others. They stress the importance of empathy. They emphasize how important it is to be open to other viewpoints and to listen to others' opinions, especially the opinions of those with whom you disagree. Perhaps most importantly, they suggest that resilience comes from caring for yourself (p. 117).

Similarly, Monroe (interview, 1998) mentioned educators' tendency not to take care of themselves. She said:

> Most of us are workaholics. We don't have a concept of time. We just do the work because it needs to be done. We work nights and weekends. But at some point you have to have enough self-knowledge and restraint to say: "It's time. That's enough." Those of us who burn out don't hear the voice inside that is saying: "You need to stop for awhile and take care of yourself."

6. *Transformed educators, schools, and systems know that learning is their lifeblood.* Learning as the core of the journey is the ultimate motivation of the individual educator, school, or system. In any transformed system, every student, teacher, administrator, district leader, community member, and parent has a passion for learning. They actively seek new knowledge and skills. They unequivocally support the need for ongoing professional development. They back this support with time, resources, and a clear understanding of research-based staff development practices. They realize that learning is essential for the life of all living systems. They realize that both individuals and organizations have the capacity to learn. They reach out to the educational knowledge base and recognize the value of open information flow and feedback. As Gregorc (interview, 1998) notes, transformed educators and school communities acknowledge that "they can learn from everyone and every thing."

Sparks (1994) proposes that at least 5 percent of a teacher's work time be spent in professional learning activities and working with peers on improving curriculum and instruction. At the 1990 ASCD Annual Conference, Bruce Joyce suggested a new set of norms for professional learning. He proposed that study be "an integral part of teachers' work; that research on effective teaching and staff development practice is possible and relevant; that public, collaborative behavior in schools is normal; and, most importantly, that teachers in schools like these are able to change students' learning rates and capabilities." Calling for built-in teacher study and collaborative work time "does not mean we embrace a deficit view of staff development," Joyce noted. "It means that to study what you do and try to become better at it is a norm of the teaching profession." Joyce stated that 10–20 percent of teachers' time should be devoted to professional growth and study.

7. *Transformed educators, schools, and systems know that one act of courage can change the world.* The essence of the heroic educator, school, and system is the courage to take unprecedented action. Heroic schools and systems confront fear head on and, like the mythic heroes of all time, find within themselves the courage to slay the dragons of ignorance, apathy, isolation, and despair. Everyone in the heroic system assumes the mantle of personal responsibility to make their dreams for children a reality.

As Stephanie Pace Marshall (1998) suggests:

> It is clear that a large part of the story that we had so logically written about human systems and human organizations—and places called schools—are grounded in false and disabling assumptions about human beings and our learning, and they are casting a malignant shadow over the human spirit. The story must simply be rewritten . . . a new story that celebrates the dynamic nature of learning and life itself.

Heroic educators collectively take responsibility for rewriting the story of their schools.

Transformation and the Heroic Educator

In *The Miracle Worker,* William Gibson creates a powerful image of the heroic teacher in his description of Annie Sullivan, tutor to Helen Keller:

> My heart is singing for joy this morning. A miracle has happened! The light of understanding has shone upon my pupil's mind, and behold, all things are changed! (Gibson, cited in Sullivan, 1996, p. 14)

When our students learn, we are filled with exhilaration. When they—or we—fail, we experience despair. The lonely, challenging, and courageous nature of the journey for teachers is captured by William Lyon Phelps in *Teachers: A Tribute:*

> The teacher can consult outside of hours with his superiors or colleagues; he can get advice and talk over his difficulties. But when he goes into the classroom, shuts the door . . . and looks into the shining morning faces, then he is thrown back absolutely on himself. No power on earth can help him, and nothing can save the situation if he makes a blunder. There he needs all his resources, all his courage, and infinite patience. (Phelps, cited in Sullivan, 1996, p. 23)

As Ginott says in *Teachers: A Tribute*: "Teachers are expected to reach unattainable goals with inadequate tools. The miracle is that at times they accomplish this impossible task." (cited in Sullivan, 1996, p. 23)

Heroic educators are deeply aware that "we teach who we are."

In *The Courage to Teach*, Palmer (1998, p. 1) states: "We teach who we are." He explains:

> Teaching, like any truly human activity, emerges from one's inwardness. . . . As I teach, I project the condition of my soul onto my students, my subject, and our way of being together. . . . Teaching holds a mirror to the soul. If I am willing to look in the mirror and not run from what I see, I have a chance to gain self-knowledge—and knowing myself is as crucial to good teaching as knowing my students and my subject. . . . When I do not know myself, I cannot know who my students are. I will see them through a glass darkly, in the shadows of my unexamined life—and when I cannot see them clearly, I cannot teach them well. When I do not know myself, I cannot know my subject—not at the deepest levels of embodied personal meaning. (p. 2)

Although Palmer makes specific reference to teachers when he says, "We teach who we are," this concept applies equally to leaders of teachers, or leaders of leaders. Thus, we can also say, "We *lead* who we are." The role of the leader in an educational system, whether a teacher team leader, a principal, or a district-level administrator, is to lead by example, to lead by teaching, to lead by supporting, and to lead by being a "lead learner."

Thus, when we lead who we are, we practice what we *say* we want others to do. And there is harmony and alignment between our espoused values and the values we live out each day in our interactions with others. Thus, if we believe that all students can learn, we also show by word and action that we believe all teachers can learn, all parents can learn, and all community members can learn. The centrality of learning is the basis of everything we do, every decision we make. The question we ask ourselves and the criterion we use for each decision is: Does this action support or obstruct teaching and learning?

Good teaching and good leading are heroic journeys to self-knowledge. The heroic educator is deeply self-aware. The epic journey of transforming schools is personal and moral. Palmer (1998) eloquently expresses this concept:

> After three decades of trying to learn my craft, every class comes down to this: my students and I, face to face, engaged in an ancient and exacting exchange called education. The techniques I have mastered do not disappear, but neither do they suffice. Face to face with my students, only one resource is at my immediate command: my identity, my selfhood, my sense of this "I" who teaches—without which I have no sense of the "Thou" who learns. . . . Good teaching cannot be reduced to technique; good teaching comes from the identity and integrity of the teacher. (p. 10)

The strong sense of personal identity that infuses their work is one hallmark of heroic educators. Palmer (1998) cites stories from his students: "'Dr. A is really *there* when she teaches' . . . or 'Mr. B. has such enthusiasm for his subject' . . . or 'You can tell that this is really Prof. C's life.'" Palmer continues:

> Good teachers possess a capacity for connectedness. They are able to weave a complex web of connections among themselves, their subjects, and their students so that students can

learn to weave a world for themselves. The methods used by these weavers vary widely: lectures, Socratic dialogues, laboratory experiments, collaborative problem solving, creative chaos. The connections made by good teachers are held not in their methods but in their hearts—meaning heart in the ancient sense, as the place where the intellect and emotion and spirit and will converge in the human self. (p. 11)

Anthony Gregorc, in his 1998 interview, echoed Palmer's words:

> The legacy of heroic educators is that they live an authentic life and are a model to others of what it means to live authentically. Thus, if a heroic system is a collection of heroic individuals, then that system would be one that looked and felt and acted in an authentic manner. It would be true to itself.

Heroic educators measure themselves against high standards.

In the transformed school, heroic educators will measure themselves against the expectations set forth by the National Board of Professional Teaching Standards (NBPTS). Here are the five propositions of the NBPTS, synthesized to a short list:

1. ***Teachers are committed to students and their learning.*** Excellent teachers are able to recognize individual differences in their students and adjust their practices accordingly. It also means that teachers treat students equitably and have a deep understanding of how students develop and learn. Finally, excellent teachers have a sense of mission that extends beyond developing the cognitive capacity of their students. They teach the whole child.

2. ***Teachers know the subjects they teach and how to teach those subjects to students.*** Excellent teachers appreciate how knowledge in their subjects is created, organized, and linked to other disciplines. They have the specific pedagogical skills needed to convey a subject to students, and they are able to generate multiple paths to knowledge.

3. ***Teachers are responsible for managing and monitoring student learning.*** Excellent teachers know how to orchestrate learning in group settings. They place a premium on student engagement. They have multiple methods to meet

their goals, and alternative ways to assess their students' progress.

4. *Teachers think systematically about their practice and learn from experience.* Because teachers are constantly making difficult choices that test their professional judgment, excellent teachers seek the advice of others and draw on education research and scholarship to improve their practice.

5. *Teachers are members of learning communities.* Excellent teachers contribute to school effectiveness by collaborating with other professionals. They work collaboratively with parents. And they seek multiple ways to learn, including networking across schools and districts, being active in professional associations, and engaging in independent and collaborative action research.

Heroic educators assume leadership roles.

In *Awakening the Sleeping Giant,* Marilyn Katzenmeyer and Gayle Moller (1996) suggest that leadership is not limited to a select group of teachers or master teachers. "If schools are to improve," they say, "all teachers must develop professional expertise, including leadership skills" (p. 12). Teachers who are leaders will lead within and beyond the classroom, influence others toward improved educational practice, and contribute to a community of teacher leaders. "As we define teacher leadership," they say, "all teachers are engaged in leadership activities to reach the goal of building a community of teacher leaders" (p. 6).

Principals in transformed schools support teacher leaders by inspiring a shared vision, enabling them to act, modeling the way, and encouraging the heart (Kouzes & Posner, 1987). Perhaps the most important role principals—and district-level administrators—can play is to embrace and enact a new paradigm for staff development. Speaking of principals in "cutting-edge" schools, Katzenmeyer and Moller (1996) note:

> They do not focus on single activities; they . . . use every available resource to provide the teachers in their schools with opportunities to lead, learn, and develop on the job. . . . Teachers in these schools become trainers of other teachers after they learn and practice new approaches . . . Teams of teachers visit

other schools to learn new strategies . . . Study groups explore topics of interest. Teachers and administrators learn together. . . . All types of learning take place, both formally and informally. (p. 29)

The role of the principal in the transformed school is to support professional community by creating the structures and time for teaming, advocating for small school size, and for school-based authority to act (Newmann & Wehlage, 1995). Heroic principals are architects of a school culture that supports the progress of all people in the school on their unique path toward growth, on their own heroic journey.

Transformation and the Heroic School and School System

Systems get changed in a thousand different ways every day. People begin doing new things and taking responsibility for unprecedented, heroic action. Systems don't change because strong leaders say "Change." They change because the leaders create conditions to support groups of people inside and on the edges to begin doing things differently (Fullan, personal communication, 1997). In transformed schools and systems, educators understand the rich and continually expanding research base on educational change. They take this knowledge and creatively use it in ways that fit the needs of their own unique setting.

Transformed schools and educational systems are communities of caring.

Communities of caring believe that children need environments in which their whole being—intellectual, emotional, spiritual, and ethical—is given a chance to grow and develop to its utmost potential. Educators in these settings believe that schools and communities must become partners to rear whole children capable of leading responsible, caring, fulfilling, and productive lives (Schaps, Lewis, & Watson, 1997).

Educators within transformed schools and educational systems understand that the professional context in which teachers work has a profound effect on their ability to respond to the needs of an increasingly diverse student population.

A five-year longitudinal study of 16 high schools in Michigan and California conducted by Stanford University professors Milbrey

Figure 8.2
Embedded Contexts That Affect Teaching

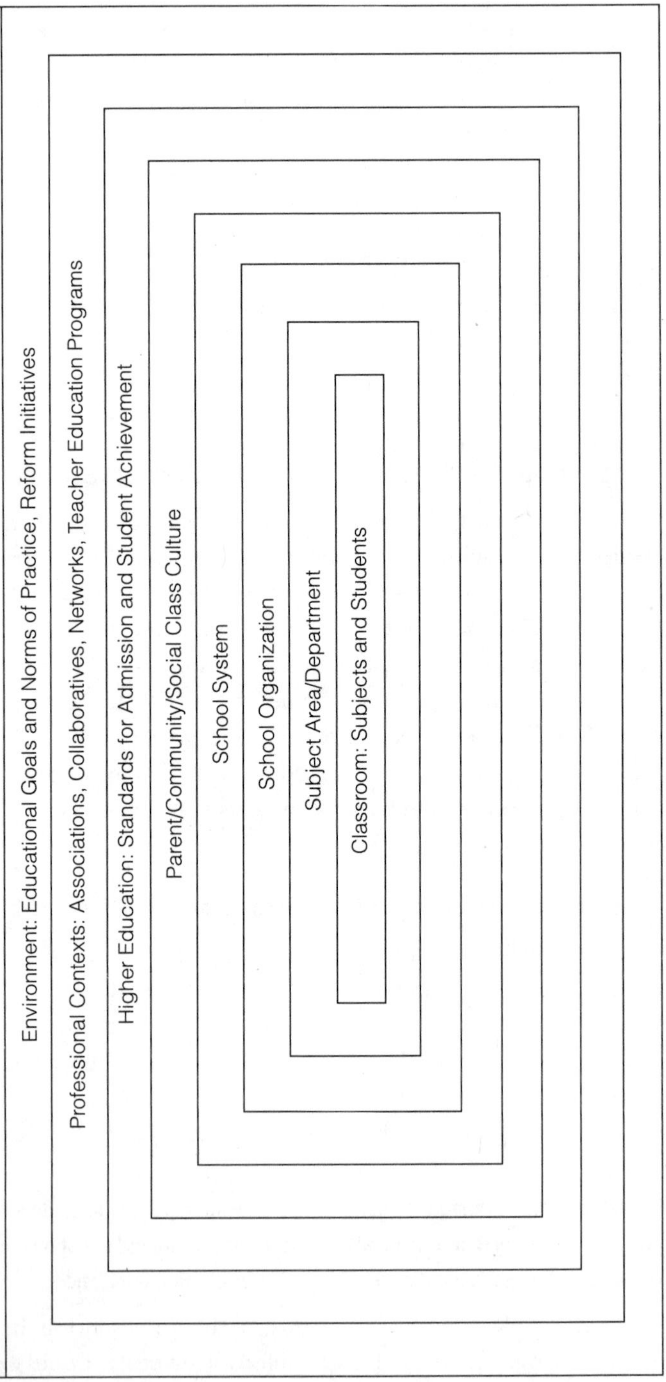

Environment: Educational Goals and Norms of Practice, Reform Initiatives

Professional Contexts: Associations, Collaboratives, Networks, Teacher Education Programs

Higher Education: Standards for Admission and Student Achievement

Parent/Community/Social Class Culture

School System

School Organization

Subject Area/Department

Classroom: Subjects and Students

McLaughlin and Joan Talbert (1993) focused on how the multiple embedded contexts (Figure 8.2) of the education system constrain and enable our goals for teaching and learning. The study found that differences in successful and unsuccessful schools (in terms of achievement, attendance, and dropout rates) were directly attributable to the presence of a context of "professional community" among teachers. Whether at the department level, the school level, or the district level, the most effective teachers had connected with a network of professionals who addressed problems and found solutions together.

The study found that strong professional communities of teachers were able to successfully adapt to demanding student populations by

• sharing responsibility for students and working together to support them;

• establishing the norm that all students can master challenging content;

• generating and sharing knowledge of effective teaching practices in the content areas; and

• engaging in ongoing assessment of their teaching practices.

In contrast, the study found that teachers who worked in a context of isolation were *least able* to meet the learning needs of a demanding student population. Most telling in the study was the effect of the school district context on teacher success. The study found that a positive district-level professional context had a positive effect on teachers even when the professional culture of their own schools was weak. Conversely, even a strong principal and active school community could not entirely overcome the influence of a weak district-level professional culture. The message is clear. Professional development, professional networking, and the active, deliberate development of professional learning communities at the school and district level are the hallmark of transformed educational systems.

The staff of transformed schools and educational systems are experts at change.

Having internalized the research base, staff members understand the proposition that change occurs one educator at a time, one school at a time, one district at a time. There is no magic bullet, no one-size-fits-all remedy. Instead, heroic systems are able to create a shared sense of the compelling need for change and to provide abundant technical assistance and support along the way.

The proposition that change occurs one educator at a time, one school at a time, is important. Bennett told us in a 1998 interview:

> I think you need to remind people not to try to duplicate or replicate what other people do. I think you can look at the major threads that they paid attention to that enhanced their chances of being successful. But I think we have to be careful not to take something wholesale because it worked somewhere else and import it directly into our own school or district without first considering the fit. I think there are lots of doors to go through. But for whatever door we choose to go through, we'd better be serious about understanding how classrooms improve, how schools improve, and teachers learn, and the process of change, and systemic learning, and how those five areas interact and intersect. And once those are in place, we begin to make wise decisions about what particular approaches we are going to design for our kids.

❖ ❖ ❖

If there were one great treasure at the end of the heroic journey in education, one shining jewel, it would be the depth and breadth of the constantly expanding knowledge base on teaching and educational change. It is a treasure more precious than gold—and one that is well within our grasp to seize and to act on.

Issues surrounding change and the complexity of the current educational reform agenda often touch people at the core of their being—their belief system. When belief systems differ, conversation becomes more difficult, and constructive dialogue often becomes impossible. In this book, we have suggested that the metaphor of the hero's journey can serve as a catalyst by virtue of its universality. As a catalyst, it can inspire thoughtful dialogue, promote common ground, and diffuse polarization in complex conversations about matters of deep importance, where widespread agreement does not exist.

We believe that the metaphor of the hero's journey, found in the stories and myths of cultures and civilizations around the world, transcends time and space and touches us at our emotional, moral, and spiritual core. In so doing, it helps us become more aware of the things that unite, rather than divide us—and provides a sense of shared experience at the deepest levels of being. Building on this sense of shared experience, diverse school communities can become capable of creating a new, more inclusive, and compelling vision for schools. And most important, we can become united in our belief in the urgency for translating that vision into action.

Heroes take journeys, confront dragons, and discover the treasure of their true selves. Although at times they may feel alone in their quests, at the end their reward is a sense of community with themselves and with others. This book is an affirmation of hope—an affirmation that through the courage of personal responsibility, shared vision, inquiry, and collective action, educators and the public can work together to find answers to the profound problems facing schools today. Above all, it is a reminder that in the collective wisdom of myth, legend, and metaphor, we can find the inspiration for a heroic journey, a journey that can be the destiny of all of us today who care deeply about our children—the children who will be the future heroes of our world.

Thus, the journey ends—and like all great journeys, its ending is also its beginning. The power of the hero's journey in education is embodied in the question that Stephanie Pace Marshall asked educators in her 1998 ASCD Annual Conference General Session in San Antonio:

> Is the work that I have described—the liberation of the genius and goodness of all children—the creation of the new mind for the new millennium, and the creation of learning communities that invite the wonder and awe of the human spirit—is *this* the work that you want to do? If so, I tell you: This is not the age of information. I repeat, this is not the age of information. This is the age of loaves and fishes. The people are hungry. And one good word, one good story, would be bread for thousands.

EPILOGUE

COMING FULL CIRCLE

───────────

As the old story goes, a discouraged and despondent educator went to see a "medium" to contact the ghost of John Dewey. When the ghost appeared, the educator said, "Professor Dewey, help me. My colleagues and I want to transform all of our schools into shining examples of learning. Is there anything you can do to assist us?"

Dewey's ghost responded, "Well, I could do it the ordinary way, or I could do it the miraculous way. Which do you prefer?"

The educator said, "Let's try the ordinary way."

At that, Dewey instantly dispatched a legion of 10,000 angels, who descended from the heavens and alighted on every school in the land, transforming them into shining temples of learning.

"Amazing!" said the educator. "That was truly amazing. But could you tell me, Professor, what is the miraculous way?"

Dewey's ghost responded, "If you would do it yourselves."

❖ ❖ ❖

How can heroic educators, schools, and systems "do it themselves" where educational transformation is concerned? That is the heart of this book. In a practical sense, we recommend that educators use the ideas and strategies presented here in a variety of settings and contexts. Some of them might include:

• ***Strategic Planning:*** School-based and district staffs can use the metaphor of the hero's journey as a facilitation tool in strategic planning sessions to create a shared vision and practical action plans; build commitment to a vision that already exists; and initiate a rapid response to complex problems where no coordinating group, common language, or shared vision now exists.

• ***Self-Reflection:*** Individual educators and school-based staffs can incorporate the questions presented in the "Reflection Checkpoints" throughout the text as a vehicle for self-study in job-embedded staff development sessions.

• ***Staff Development:*** Educators can incorporate our suggested strategies and processes into a variety of professional development experiences: study groups, school-based staff development sessions, partner dialogues, community forums, and professional development workshops focused on change facilitation skills. In particular, the metaphors presented here can assist staffs in solving problems, breaking out of either/or thinking, seeing problems and opportunities in a new light, and investigating the collective path of school and educational renewal.

• ***Vision Setting:*** Above all, we believe that the ideas presented here can reinforce educators' efforts to develop informed consensus, based on research and practice, on a bold new vision for schools and the immediate steps needed to achieve it.

❖ ❖ ❖

Shortly before his death in 1987, Joseph Campbell participated in a series of interviews with Bill Moyers, prominent Public Broadcasting Service journalist and writer. The conversations took place at George Lucas's Skywalker Ranch in California. The interview transcripts were edited into the book *The Power of Myth* (Campbell & Moyers, 1988). In that book, Moyers notes the following:

> Walking to work one morning after Campbell's death, I stopped
> before a neighborhood video store that was showing scenes

from George Lucas' *Star Wars* on a monitor in the window. I stood there thinking of the time Campbell and I had watched the movie together at Lucas' Skywalker Ranch in California.

Campbell reveled in the ancient themes and motifs of mythology unfolding on the wide screen in powerful contemporary images. On this particular visit, having again exulted over the perils and heroics of Luke Skywalker, Joe grew animated as he talked about how Lucas "has put the newest and most powerful spin" to the classic story of the hero.

"And what is that?" I asked.

"It's what Goethe said in *Faust* but which Lucas has dressed in modern idiom—the message that technology is not going to save us. Our computers, our tools, our machines are not enough. We have to rely on our intuition, our true being."

"Isn't that an affront to reason?" I said.

"That's not what the hero's journey is about," Campbell responded. "It's not to deny reason. To the contrary, by overcoming dark passions, the hero symbolizes our ability to control the irrational savage within us."

Campbell was describing the hero's journey not as a courageous act but as a life lived in self-discovery, "and Luke Skywalker was never more rational than when he found within himself the resources of character to meet his destiny," Campbell said.

To Campbell, the end of the hero's journey is "not the aggrandizement of the hero. . . . The ultimate aim of the quest must be neither release nor ecstasy for oneself, but the wisdom and the power to serve others." One of the many distinctions between the celebrity and the hero, he said, is that one lives only for self while the other acts to redeem society. (pp. xiii–xiv)

"In that sense," I said, "unlike heroes such as Prometheus, we're not going on our journey to save the world but to save ourselves." Campbell's response was: "But in doing that, you save the world. The influence of a vital person vitalizes. The world without spirit is a wasteland." (p. 183)

Appendix A

Interview Guides

Overview

We are at a crossroads in education that calls for nothing less than heroism on the part of individuals and organizations if public education is to survive. To be heroic, either as an individual or as a school organization, is to accept the responsibility and to sustain the commitment (despite both external obstacles and tests of internal fortitude) for confronting and resolving the critical problems that are facing education today. The times demand that we act with courage, vision, integrity, moral purpose, and extraordinary caring for both our colleagues and the children we serve. We believe we are up to the task.

We suggest that great personal and institutional transformation inevitably requires educators to confront a series of distinct but intricately interconnected phases of an archetypal "heroic journey." This process is similar to journeys taken in story, myth, and legend by heroic figures like Odysseus, Dante, Parzival, Joan of Arc, Buddha, Siddhartha, Black Elk, Arjuna (in the *Bhagavad Gita*), Bilbo Baggins, Dorothy (in *The Wizard of Oz*), and Luke Skywalker (in *Star Wars*), as well as the lives of heroic historical figures like Martin Luther King, Mother Teresa, and Ghandi.

The metaphor of the heroic journey is so universal that it enables even highly polarized groups to find common ground, identify shared purpose, and reach consensus on informed action. Metaphor has the

---

Authors' note: We distributed materials in this appendix in advance to the people we interviewed for this book. In our conversations, they responded to the interview questions from their own experiences. We invite readers to adapt the Overview and three sets of Interview Questions for their own use.

power to kindle the imagination and touch the heart. In so doing, it can help members of a diverse school community become more aware of the things that unite them, rather than what divides them. The result is often a higher level of creative thinking on the part of teams and a commitment to translating plans into action.

Interview Questions Used for This Book

Each stage of the journey lends itself to questions that will be the focus of this interview.

1. *Innocence Lost: Breakdown Requires Breakthrough*

What are the outmoded or self-deceptive mindsets and barriers that keep educators and schools from moving forward? What in your personal experience in education represents a state of innocence to which we can never return? How do organizational paradigms, policies, and structural components keep schools from becoming heroic?

2. *Chaos and Complexity This Way Come: Confronting the Dragon at the Door and the Serpent in the Garden*

What problems and undeclared realities make it imperative that we embark on the heroic journey? What is forcing us today to take our heads out of the sand? What is the nature of the dragon at the door and the serpent in the garden? (For the individual educator, the school, and the system?)

3. *The Heroic Quest: The Search for the Grail, the Jewel in the Lotus, and Avalon*

What is the vision that needs to drive our action? What is the relationship between personal and collective (or shared) vision? How do we become reconnected and one with our vision—as educators and as schools? How do we hold on to our vision when the going gets tough?

4. *Gurus and Alliances: Companions Along the Way*

Who are the gurus that influence us and why? How does knowledge from without (embodied in the work of educational researchers, theorists, and nationally recognized educators) get successfully translated into knowledge and wisdom within? How can we tap into the collective wisdom that resides within both ourselves and our schools, rather than only looking outward for the "savior," the panacea, or the scapegoat? Who are our companions along the way? How do they sustain us?

5. *Trials, Tests, and Initiations: Staying the Course*

How can we maintain our internal resolve, resiliency, and emotional intelligence in the face of problems and barriers resulting from the quest for transformation? How can we develop mechanisms to cope with the inevitable problems and conflict that accompany change? How do we confront these problems with creativity and hope? What are the external barriers that are blocking our way, and how can we take individual and collective responsibility for overcoming them? How do we avoid placing the blame and the responsibility on others? How do we prevent overload, burnout, and backsliding into our comfort zone?

6. *Insight and Transformation: Arriving Where We Started and Knowing the Place for the First Time*

What are the characteristics of a transformed educator, school, and system? Why is the end always a beginning? When do we really "get there," and what does "it" look like? Based on what we learn on our journey, what are the guiding principles and what is the legacy that we can offer to others as they embark on similar quests?

Interview Questions for Use with School Improvement Teams

School improvement teams can use these questions (and the Overview) as a tool to facilitate self-assessment and purposeful dialogue as they embark on the journey of comprehensive school improvement planning.

1. *Innocence Lost: Breakdown Requires Breakthrough*

What are the old mindsets that represent a state of "innocence" as we begin our journey of school improvement planning? How have we experienced mindsets, such as "This too shall pass," "If only someone else would . . . ."? What realities about teaching, learning, school, and life in the next century can we no longer deny?

2. *Chaos and Complexity This Way Come: Confronting the Dragon at the Door and the Serpent in the Garden*

What are the realities that make it imperative that we embark on a heroic journey of school improvement? When we choose to begin this journey, what is the nature of the complexity we will face? What will feel chaotic and why? What "dragons" will we need to face and overcome?

3. *The Heroic Quest: The Search for the Grail, the Jewel in the Lotus, and Avalon*

What are the values about teaching, learning, and school that need to drive our action? What is our vision, or the object of our quest? As individuals and organizations, what is the "treasure" we are seeking?

4. *Gurus and Alliances: Companions Along the Way*

Who are the wisdom figures who can guide us in our journey? From whom can and must we learn? Who are our mentors? Who are our traveling companions along the way? How do they sustain us?

5. *Trials, Tests, and Initiations: Staying the Course*

How can we maintain our internal resolve, resiliency, and emotional intelligence in the face of problems and barriers? What are the amulets and shields that can help us? How can we (as individuals and organizations) develop the capability to confront—with creativity and hope—the inevitable problems that accompany change? How do we prevent overload, burnout, and backsliding into our comfort zone?

6. *Insight and Transformation: Arriving Where We Started and Knowing the Place for the First Time*

What is the treasure at the journey's end? What is the gift that we bring to those whom we serve? Based on what we learn on our journey, what are the guiding principles and what is the legacy that we can offer to others as they embark on similar quests?

Interview Questions for Staff Developers

School and district staff developers can use these questions (and the Overview) as a tool to facilitate self-assessment and purposeful dialogue in a variety of professional development settings. These questions can facilitate "staff development for staff developers"—and can set the climate for collaborative inquiry, problem solving, and job-embedded staff development. In this way, we can promote the capacity to transform schools into communities of caring and increased professionalism for the adults who work in them.

1. *Innocence Lost: Breakdown Requires Breakthrough*

In what ways have you demonstrated a state of "innocence" in your role as a staff developer? What are the outmoded mindsets that you have confronted among participants in your recent staff development sessions?

2. *Chaos and Complexity This Way Come: Confronting the Dragon at the Door and the Serpent in the Garden*

What are the "dragons" and "serpents" in your current role as a staff developer? How do these embodiments of chaos and complexity affect staff development in your district?

3. *The Heroic Quest: The Search for the Grail, the Jewel in the Lotus, and Avalon*

What is the "treasure" you are seeking as a staff developer? Despite the chaos and complexity you confront, what is the vision that sustains you in your professional role?

4. *Gurus and Alliances: Companions Along the Way*

Who are the wisdom figures who guide you in your role as staff developer? What are the possible pitfalls and dangers in over-reliance on external consultants in staff development? What is the role of the mentor in staff development? How can we use the power of collaborative inquiry, networking, and action research to promote the success of our staff development initiatives? How do these processes enhance job-embedded staff development?

5. *Trials, Tests, and Initiations: Staying the Course*

How can we maintain our internal resolve, resiliency, and emotional intelligence in the face of problems and barriers resulting from the quest for transformational staff development? How can we confront—with creativity and hope—the inevitable problems that accompany change? How do we prevent overload, burnout, and backsliding into our comfort zone?

6. *Insight and Transformation: Arriving Where We Started and Knowing the Place for the First Time*

What is our legacy as staff developers? What is the treasure that we bring to those whom we serve and with whom we work?

Appendix B

Perspectives from Real Life in Education

Here, we share some tangible examples of heroic educators, schools, and systems in action as they move through the stages of the hero's journey. The following represent real individuals and institutions with whom we have worked. We hope you will recognize aspects of yourself and your life experiences in these examples.

Breakdown and the Call: Innocence Lost

In our experience, the most obvious sign that an educator or staff are in the "Innocence Lost" phase of the journey is a pervasive sense of world-weariness, fatigue, or alienation. One high school teacher, for example, appeared almost detached and emotionless when confronted with a new high school assessment program imposed by the state. His few comments on this accountability initiative centered around two themes we've heard from other teachers: "We've done this stuff before," and "This will eventually go away, like everything else the state does." It was only when the accountability stakes became so huge—and his professional survival became imperiled—that he began to move out of innocence into acknowledging the chaos and complexity that were defining his life.

Innocence Lost is typically a stage of denial and deep unconsciousness. Within a school building or system, we see evidence of it whenever we find entrenched, intractable behaviors that are so deeply institutionalized that they allow for no flexibility in the face of change and discord. Several principals with whom we have worked, for example, dig in their heels and become virtually autocratic when the forces of external or internal change confront them and their staffs.

Typically, they cling to policies and procedures as totem figures, failing miserably to rally their staffs and build consensus about immediate and long-range priorities. When schools or school systems are run this way—with top-down mandates and little if any collaboration to ease the process toward transformation—there is an inevitability about their remaining fixed in the land of Innocence, with a resulting rigidity and inability to confront the realities of the world confronting them.

We can think of no more powerful example of a school icebound in the Land of Innocence than one site where we consulted. During our time there, the faculty was friendly and accessible, but determined to resist any institutional or organizational changes until the system "dealt with the problems that most of our kids bring to school with them." Staff members lamented: "We can't develop new programs, mount new schedules, or change instruction until the system gets them to come to school ready to learn." These kinds of attitudes are the hallmarks of Innocence, an innocence that must, inevitably, be lost if the school and its stakeholders are to move forward to help students fully prepare for a changing world.

Chaos and Complexity This Way Come

We have seen that when heroic educators face the dragons and serpents of change, they awaken from a false sense of innocence to confront the monsters and demons knocking on their doors. But in the resulting "Chaos and Complexity," many educators experience a sense of anxiety, fear, or defensiveness. "What are we possibly going to do?" many may cry. "This looks impossible . . . overwhelming . . . more than we can handle."

These variations typify the reactions to chaos and complexity among educators with whom we have worked in a variety of intense, change-driven settings. Whenever such educators discover the internal resources to confront the challenges facing them, however, we begin to see evidence of their transformation from *chaos* to *questing*—that is, we see the emergence of the heroic quest.

Similarly, many schools with which we have worked initially *dissemble* before *reassembling* to confront either internal or external change forces. One middle school staff, for example, spent two years either denying that a state-mandated performance assessment test had any validity—or complaining about how inadequately prepared their students were to address such demanding intellectual tasks. The norms at this school during its Chaos and Complexity stage were typified by high levels of anxiety, apprehension, and feelings of incompetence and resentment. At the end of the two years—after a new principal arrived and the staff had instituted a process of staff-based action research to investigate how *they as a staff* could solve their assessment and student achievement problems—the staff began to realize its own power and efficacy. As a result, they moved as a group out of chaos into the search for heroic solutions.

The Heroic Quest: The Search for the Grail

When considering the Heroic Quest, we often think of several educators to whom we have remained close through the years after working with them in a consulting or advisory capacity. These teachers and administrators all share one common characteristic: *They have a vision and deep sense of purpose*—and they are more than willing to share both with everyone with whom they come in contact. When educators have fully embarked on the heroic quest, they can quickly and authentically share the nature of the grail, jewel in the lotus, or magical ring for which they are questing. Just as inevitably, those educators confirm, to a person, that their quest involves working to transform the well-being and lifelong success of the students they serve.

Similarly, the most successful elementary, middle, and high school sites we know embody the heroic quest as a fundamental part of their organizational culture. You can see it when you walk into the building:

- A vision and mission statement are clearly evident.
- Physical icons and artifacts from student performances are everywhere in the school.
- Teachers, administrators, students, and parents all can articulate with great agreement what it is that makes their school a great place to learn and work.

All schools and school systems in this phase of the journey have a clear sense of purpose, a real commitment to a vision for students, and a collaborative spirit in which everyone moves together toward common strategic ends.

Gurus and Alliances: Companions Along the Way

Current educational research emphasizes the power of collaboration, shared inquiry, and collective decision making and problem solving. Like all of the phases of the hero's journey, however, paradoxes abound here, too: Educators can have false or naive expectations of gurus and alliances, or educators and schools can empower themselves through alliances and companions.

In our roles as consultants and facilitators to schools and systems, we have found that the "guru phenomenon" is alive and well in education. We have known some middle and high school sites, endowed with either generous district budgets for staff development or internally generated grants, to engage many consultants and external advisors. Usually, if the school becomes excessively dependent on a particular "wisdom figure" or facilitator, they remain in a kind of lost innocence, assuming that this expert will do the job for them. With a deep level of unconsciousness, such staffs raise the guru to the level of savior figure, with little if any internal ownership of the change process.

In contrast, the mature organizations with which we have worked have typically moved beyond the "guru" phase of the journey. Instead, they have discovered the power and efficacy of collaboration and shared inquiry. When a school or system is truly at this phase of the hero's journey, we see action research, study groups, and collaborative work cultures as norms, rather than outliers. Gurus or consultants play a role here, but the heroes and heroines of the transformed school have internalized and constructed meaning on their own. They make use of the wisdom of these gurus as guideposts, not ideologies.

Trials, Tests, and Initiations

People at this phase of the journey are almost inevitably confronted with some variation of the "dark night of the soul." Many of the best teachers and administrators with whom we have worked find themselves at some form of crossroads during their careers. Their trials and tests almost always consist of a reexamination of the purpose of their career, a sense of self-doubt about what they have accomplished during that career, or a nagging sense that other challenges are tempting them to deviate from their course and embark on a new journey.

At the same time, we have seen many heroic educators and administrators at this phase of the journey riddled with self-doubts about their capacity for dealing with contemporary educational problems and realities. We have heard some of the best and brightest question their ability to deal with "the new media-generation student," the realities of urban and suburban violence and student apathy, the real impact of two-parent workers within households, and the growing realities of students who no longer appear to respect authority just for the sake of respecting it.

This phase almost inevitably involves enormous upheaval or overwhelming change forces at the school and system levels. We can easily recognize a school or system at the "Trial, Test, and Initiation" stage of the journey whenever organizational climates and cultures exhibit a preponderance of anxiety, fear, and uncertainty. The best elementary, middle, and high school sites with which we have worked seem to recognize that they are never *not* in this phase. In effect, every day is a series of trials, tests, and initiations.

Blue Ribbon Schools and other award-winning sites empower their staffs to work together to solve problems and make decisions. Moreover, every successful heroic school depends on an organic process of strategic planning for student achievement. Anticipating and planning strategically for the bumps and bruises that will inevitably confront schools and systems are powerful tools and amulets—and are highly evident in sites successfully addressing this phase of the journey.

Insight and Transformation: Arriving Where We Started and Knowing the Place for the First Time

The best teachers and administrators we have had the privilege to know recognize that the journey in education is always *elliptical and recursive*. It never ends, because in the end is a new beginning. The "Insight and Transformation" phase of the journey finds experienced educators enthusiastically sharing their experience and expertise with others, particularly the beginning teachers who will replace the enormous numbers of educators who entered the profession in the late '60s and '70s. These transformed educators embody the quest and the excitement that accompanies it. They engage in mentoring, peer coaching, study groups, and related forms of consensus building and inquiry.

Similarly, transformed schools and school systems embody similar insights, values, and practices. In the transformed schools with which we have worked, the faculty, students, parents, and community members work closely together to learn from one another. Shared decision making and problem solving are not artificial exercises but real organizational practices. Professional development does not consist of big-ticket, one-shot workshops, but an ongoing process of shared learning, investigation, and action research. Governance and management, similarly, exemplify norms of collegiality and collective empowerment; and administrators and others in leadership positions recognize the inevitable phases through which the adult learner must move to internalize an innovation or change element.

❖ ❖ ❖

Ultimately, the hero's journey in education is a shared experience. It is an ongoing event, a process in which the new and the old, the seasoned and uninitiated, work together toward a common set of purposes. It is the journey, not the destination, that we all share as part of the heroic quest in education.

References

Bailey, S. (1996, March). Forging unified commitments from diverse perspectives: New approaches to helping groups through change [ASCD Professional Development Institute], San Francisco.

Barell, J. (1991). *Teaching for thoughtfulness: Classroom strategies to enhance intellectual growth.* New York: Longman.

Barth, R. (1990). *Improving schools from within.* San Francisco: Jossey-Bass.

Baum, L. F. (1996). *The Wizard of Oz.* New York: North-South Books.

Berman. P., & McLaughlin, M. (1977). *Federal programs supporting educational change: Vol. VIII. Implementing and sustaining innovations.* Santa Monica, CA: Rand.

Block, P. (1987). *The empowered manager.* San Francisco: Jossey-Bass.

Bolman, L. G., & Deal, T. E. (1995). *Leading with soul: An uncommon journey of spirit.* San Francisco: Jossey-Bass.

Bridges, W. (1991). *Managing transitions: Making the most of change.* Reading, MA: Addison-Wesley.

Caine, R. N., & Caine, G. (1991). *Making connections.* Alexandria, VA: Association for Supervision and Curriculum Development.

Campbell, J. (1949). *The hero with a thousand faces.* Princeton, NJ: Princeton University Press.

Campbell, J. (1968). *The masks of gods. Vol. 4. Creative mythology.* New York: Viking Press.

Campbell, J. (with Abadie, M. J.). (1974). *The mythic path.* Princeton, NJ: Princeton University Press.

Campbell, J., & Moyers, B. (1988). *The power of myth.* New York: Doubleday.

Costa, A., & Garmston, R. (1994). *Cognitive coaching: A foundation for renaissance schools.* Norwood, MA: Christopher Gordon.

Dante, A. (trans. and commentary by J. D. Sinclair). (1961). *Inferno.* Oxford: Oxford University Press.

Deal, T. E., & Peterson, K. D. (1999). *Shaping culture: The heart of leadership.* San Francisco: Jossey-Bass.

de Geus, A. (1997). *The living company: Habits for survival in a turbulent business environment.* Boston: Harvard Business School Press.

Eliot, T. S. (1943). *Four quartets.* San Diego: Harcourt Brace Jovanovich.

Feinstein, D., & Krippner, S. (1997). *The mythic path.* New York: Tarcher/ Putnam.

Fitzpatrick, K. (Ed.). (1998). *Indicators of schools of quality* (Vols. I & II). Schaumburg, IL: National Study for School Evaluation.

181

Forest, H. (Ed.). (1996). *Wisdom tales from around the world*. Little Rock, AR: August House.

Frazer, J. G. (1890/1994). *The golden bough*. London: Oxford University Press.

Fullan, M., & Hargreaves, A. (1991). *What's worth fighting for? Working together for your school*. Toronto and Andover, MA: Regional Laboratory for Educational Improvement of the Northeast and Islands (with Ontario Public School Teachers' Federation).

Fullan, M. (1992, February). Visions that blind. *Educational Leadership, 49*(5), 19–23.

Fullan, M. (1993a). *Change forces: Probing the depths of educational reform*. London, UK: Falmer Press.

Fullan, M. (1993b). Innovation, reform, and restructuring strategies. In G. Cawelti (Ed.), *Challenges and achievements of American education: ASCD 1993 Yearbook*. Alexandria, VA.: Association for Supervision and Curriculum Development.

Fullan, M., & Miles, M. (1992). Getting reform right: What works and what doesn't. *Phi Delta Kappan, 73*(10), 744–752.

Fullan, M. (with Stielbauer, S.). (1991). *The new meaning of educational change*. New York: Teachers College Press.

Gardner, H. (1983). *Frames of mind*. New York: Basic Books.

Gardner, H. (1991). *The unschooled mind: How children think and how schools should teach*. New York: Basic Books.

Garmston, R., & Wellman, B. (1995, April). Adaptive schools in a quantum universe. *Educational Leadership, 52*(7), 6–14.

Gleick, J. (1987). *Chaos: Making a new science*. New York: Penguin Books.

Glickman, C., Allen, L., & Lunsford, B. (1994). Factors affecting school change. *Journal of Staff Development, 15*(3), 38–41.

Goleman, D. (1995). *Emotional intelligence*. New York: Bantam Books.

Greene, M. (1997, January). Metaphors and multiples. *Phi Delta Kappan, 78*(5), 387–394.

Guskey, T., & Huberman, M. (Eds.). (1995). *Professional development in education: New paradigms and practices*. New York: Teachers College Press.

Hall, G., & Loucks, S. (1978). Teacher concerns as a basis for facilitating and personalizing staff development. *Teachers College Record, 80*(1), 36–53.

Hargreaves, A. (1997). Rethinking educational change. In A. Hargreaves (Ed.), *Rethinking educational change with heart and mind: 1997 ASCD yearbook*. Alexandria, VA: Association for Supervision and Curriculum Development.

Hargreaves, A., & Fullan, M. (1998). *What's worth fighting for out there?* New York: Teachers College Press.

Herman, J. L., Aschbacher, P. R., & Winters, L. (1992). *A practical guide to alternative assessment*. Alexandria, VA : Association for Supervision and Curriculum Development.

Herrmann, N. (1988). *The creative brain*. Lake Lure, NC: Brain Books.

Hixson, J. (1997, November). Helping school teams lead successful schoolwide change [ASCD Professional Development Institute], Boston.

Hord, S. M., Rutherford, W. L., Huling-Austin, L., & Hall, G. E. (1987). *Taking charge of change*. Alexandria, VA: Association of Supervision and Curriculum Development.

Ingvar, D. (1985). Memory of the future: An essay on the temporal organization of conscious awareness. *Human Neurobiology*, pp. 127–136.

Joyce, B. (1990, March). *Changing school culture through staff development*. Presentation at the Annual Conference of the Association for Supervision and Curriculum Development, San Antonio, TX.

Joyce, B., Wolf, J., & Calhoun, E. (1993). *The self-renewing school*. Alexandria, VA: Association for Supervision and Curriculum Development.

Jung, C. G. (1963). *Memories, dreams, reflections* (A. Jaffé, Ed.) (R. Winston & C. Winston, Trans.). New York: Pantheon.

Jung, C. G. (Ed.). (1964). *Man and his symbols*. New York: Dell.

Karp, H. (1988). A positive approach to resistance. Adapted from J. W. Pfeiffer (Ed.), *The 1988 annual: Developing human resources*. San Diego, CA: University Associates.

Katzenmeyer, M., & Moller, G. (1996). *Awakening the sleeping giant: Leadership development for teachers*. Thousand Oaks, CA: Corwin Press.

Kohn, A. (1997, September 3). Students don't work—they learn. *Education Week*, pp. 61, 43.

Kouzes, J., & Posner, B. (1987). *The leadership challenge*. San Francisco: Jossey-Bass.

Kuhn, T. S. (1962/1996). *The structure of scientific revolutions* (3rd ed.). Chicago: University of Chicago Press.

Lambert, L., Walker, D., Zimmerman, D., Cooper, J., Lambert, M. D., Gardner, M. E., & Ford-Slack, P. J. (1995). *The constructivist leader*. New York: Teachers College Press.

Lieberman, A., Darling-Hammond, L., & Zuckerman, D. (1991) *Early lessons in restructuring schools*. New York: Columbia University National Center for Restructuring Education, Schools, and Teaching.

Little, J. W. (1982). Norms of collegiality and experimentation: Workplace conditions of school success. *American Educational Research Journal, 5*(19), 325–340.

Lorenz, E. N. (1993). *The essence of chaos*. Seattle, WA : University of Washington Press.

Louis, K. S., & Miles, M. B. (1990). *Improving the urban high school: What works and why*. New York: Teachers College Press.

Marshall, S. P. (1998, March). *Leading, learning, loving, and letting go: Creating learning communities that invite and nurture intelligence, creativity, wisdom, and power of the human spirit—what is possible?* Keynote address presented at the Annual Conference of the Association for Supervision and Curriculum Development, San Antonio.

Marzano, R. (1992). *A different kind of classroom*. Alexandria, VA: Association for Supervision and Curriculum Development.

Maurer, R. (1996). *Beyond the wall of resistance*. Austin, TX: Bard Books.

McLaughlin, M. W., & Talbert, J. (1993). *Contexts that matter for teaching and learning.* Stanford, CA: Center for Research on the Context of Secondary School Teaching.

Meier, D. (1995). *The power of their ideas: Lessons for America from a small school in Harlem.* Boston: Beacon.

Micklethwait, J., & Wooldridge, A. (1996). *The witch doctors: Making sense of management gurus.* New York: Random House.

Mintzberg, H. (1994). *The rise and fall of strategic planning.* New York: Free Press.

Moffett, C. (1995a, Winter). Making time for staff development: Luxury or necessity? *The ASCD Professional Development Newsletter,* 1–2, 8.

Moffett, C. (1995b, Spring). Resistance to change: Taking a closer look. *The ASCD Professional Development Newsletter,* 1–2, 8.

Monroe, L. (1994, December). *School reform: Lessons from the field.* Keynote address presented at the annual conference of the National Staff Development Council, Orlando, Florida.

Monroe, L. (1997). *Nothing's impossible: Leadership lessons from inside and outside the classroom.* New York: New York Times Books.

Murphy, E. C. (1994). *Forging the heroic organization: A daring blueprint for revitalizing American business.* Englewood Cliffs, NJ: Prentice Hall.

Nais, J., Southworth, G., & Campbell, P. (1992). *Whole school curriculum development in the primary school.* Lewes, England: Falmer Press.

Neihardt, J. G. (1979). *Black Elk speaks.* Lincoln: University of Nebraska Press.

Newmann, F., & Wehlage, G. (1995). *Successful school restructuring.* Madison, WI: Center on Organization and Restructuring of Schools.

Palmer, P. J. (1998) *The courage to teach: Exploring the inner landscape of a teacher's life.* San Francisco: Jossey-Bass.

Pearson, C. S. (1989). *The hero within: Six archetypes we live by.* San Francisco: Harper Collins.

Pearson, C. S. (1991). *Awakening the heroes within: Twelve archetypes to help us find ourselves and transform our world.* San Francisco: Harper Collins.

Peel, J., & McCary, C. E. III. (1997, May). Visioning the "little red schoolhouse" for the 21st century. *Phi Delta Kappan, 78*(9), 702–705.

Pugh, S. (1989, Spring). Metaphor and learning. *Reading Research and Instruction, 28*(3), 19.

The quotable traveler: Wise words for travelers, explorers, and wanderers. (1994). Philadelphia: Running Press.

Rogers, E. (1991). *Diffusion of innovations.* New York: The Free Press.

Rosenholtz, S. (1989). *Teachers' workplace: The social organization of schools.* New York: Longman.

Rumi, J. (1997). *In the arms of the beloved* (Jonathan Star, Trans.). New York: Jeremy P. Tarcher/Putnam.

Saphier, J., & King, M. (1985, March). Good seeds grow in strong cultures. *Educational Leadership, 42*(6), 67–74.

Sarason, S. (1971). *The culture of the school and the problem of change.* Boston: Allyn & Bacon.

Sarason, S. (1990). *The predictable failure of educational reform: Can we change course before it's too late?* San Francisco: Jossey-Bass.

Satchidananda, S. (Trans.) (1997). *The Bhagavad Gita.* Yogaville, VA: Integral Yoga Publications.

Saxl, E., Miles, M., & Lieberman, A. (1990). *Assisting change in education.* Alexandria, VA: Association for Supervision and Curriculum Development.

Schaps, E., Lewis, C., & Watson, M. (1997, September). Building classroom communities. *Thrust for Educational Leadership, 27*(1), 14–15.

Schwartz, P. (1991) *The art of the long view.* New York: Doubleday.

Senge, P. (1990). *The fifth discipline: The art and practice of the learning organization.* New York: Doubleday.

Senge, P., Roberts, C., Ross, R., Smith, B., & Kleiner, A. (1994). *The fifth discipline fieldbook.* New York: Doubleday.

Sergiovanni, T. (1994). *Building community schools.* San Francisco: Jossey-Bass.

Sparks, D., (1994, February). Time for learning: A view from the national level. *Professional development: Changing times* (Policy Brief No. 4). Oak Brook, IL: North Central Regional Education Laboratory.

Sparks, D., & Hirsh, S. (1997). *A new paradigm for staff development.* Alexandria, VA: Association for Supervision and Curriculum Development.

Stacey, R. (1992). *Managing the unknowable.* San Francisco: Jossey-Bass.

Stacey, R. (1996). *Complexity and creativity in organizations.* San Francisco: Berrett-Koehler.

Storr, A. (Ed.). (1983). *The essential Jung.* New York: MJF Books.

Sullivan, B. (Ed.). (1996). *Teachers: A tribute.* Kansas City, MO: Andrews & McMeel.

Tigunait, P. R. (1995). *Inner quest: The path of spiritual unfoldment.* Honesdale, PA: Yoga International Books.

Vogler, C. (1998). *The writer's journey: Mythic structure for writers.* Studio City, CA: M. Wiese Productions.

Von Oech, R. (1983). *A whack on the side of the head: How to unlock your mind for innovation.* New York: Warner Books.

Vygotsky, L. S. (1962). *Thought and language.* Cambridge, MA: MIT Press.

Weisbord, M., & Janoff, S. (1995). *Future search.* San Francisco: Berrett-Koehler.

Wheatley, M. (1992). *Leadership and the new science: Learning about organization from an orderly universe.* San Francisco: Berrett-Koehler.

Wheatley, M., & Kellner-Rogers, M. (1996). *A simpler way.* San Francisco: Berrett-Koehler.

White, T. H. (1987/1996). *The once and future king.* New York: Ace Books.

Williams, L. V. (1983). *Teaching for the two-sided mind: A guide to right brain/left brain education.* Englewood Cliffs, NJ: Prentice Hall.

INDEX

About the Authors

John L. Brown is the Director of Program Development for Prince George's County Public Schools, Maryland, the 17th largest school system in the United States. In that capacity, he is responsible for overseeing all phases of curriculum design, development, and implementation, as well as new and emerging programs. He is the author of the ASCD book *Observing Dimensions of Learning in Classrooms and Schools*. Brown has also done extensive educational consulting work throughout the United States and Canada, including training in Dimensions of Learning, standards-based curriculum, learning styles, and strategic planning. He is a member of the training cohort for the ASCD program Understanding by Design. In addition, Brown has served as an adjunct professor in Curriculum Theory and Development at several colleges and universities in the Washington, D.C., area, including Johns Hopkins University, Western Maryland University, and Trinity College. In 1996, he completed his Ph.D. in Education at George Mason University, Fairfax, Virginia. He can be reached at 5659 Governor's Pond Circle, Alexandria, VA 22310. Telephone: office: 301-952-6591; home: 703-960-1707; fax: 301-952-6504..

Cerylle A. Moffett is Senior Associate for The New Standards Project at the National Center for Education and the Economy (NCEE) in Washington, D.C. As a member of ASCD's Professional Development staff for 15 years, she most recently served as ASCD Program Manager for Professional Development. Moffett is co-author of the ASCD books *Dimensions of Learning; Implementing Dimensions of Learning in Classrooms and Schools;* and *Educators Supporting Educators: A Guide to Organizing School Support Teams.* Her areas of expertise include professional development program design, delivery, and evaluation; the collaborative facilitation of change; creating values-based schools and classrooms; and implementing standards-based curriculum and instruction. As Project Coordinator for ASCD's Assisting Change in Education program, Moffett has designed and delivered staff development programs for educators across the United States and Canada, and for the Department of Defense Dependent Schools in Panama, Italy, and the Far East. She can be reached at Cerylle Moffett and Associates, 916 De Wolfe Drive, Alexandria, VA 22308. Telephone: 703-780-6502; fax: 703-780-9192; e-mail: cerylle@aol.com